Property of Ella Nora Miller   1-17-83

PITY THE POOR RICH

PITY THE POOR RICH

BERT GREENE

WITH

PHILLIP STEPHEN SCHULZ

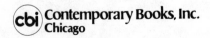 **Contemporary Books, Inc.**
Chicago

Library of Congress Cataloging in Publication Data

Greene, Bert, 1923-
  Pity the poor rich.

  Bibliography: p.
  1. Millionaires—United States.   I. Schulz, Phillip
Stephen, joint author.   II. Title.
HG172.A2G73   1978   332'.092'2   78-57451
ISBN 0-8092-8198-8

Published by Contemporary Books, Inc.
180 North Michigan Avenue, Chicago, Illinois 60601
Manufactured in the United States of America
Library of Congress Catalog Card Number: 78-57451
international Standard Book Number: 0-8092-8198-8

Published simultaneously in Canada by
Beaverbooks
953 Dillingham Road
Pickering, Ontario L1W 1Z7
Canada

CONTENTS

FOREWORD

Twelve years ago when I co-founded *The Store in Amagan-sett* with Denis Vaughan (as a talented but novice duo of chefs), the rich were our first and most enthusiastic patrons. Long before the jet-setters and the movie and TV stars became devotees, the old guard of the Hamptons (obviously bored by the lack of culinary prerogatives in the territory) arrived at our saffron-colored door to buy up little snacks for their cocktail parties.

They adored our pâté and baked ham as well. They raptured over our ziti salad, and we supplied them with enough that first summer to fill their swimming pools. But though the rich were always praiseful of our efforts (particularly those dishes we produced with confidence), they were never completely satisfied.

"You're going to be a big success out here," they would predict balefully. "But you really must *do* quiche you know. . . . "

We didn't want to do anything of the kind. But the admonition of our gilded customers (in their Puccis and Guccis) was so emphatic we dared not refuse. We learned how to make the requested quiche—aspic and *quenelle de brochet*—like troupers! And mousse (anything from salmon flavor to strawberry) became a standard, as they say in the music business. Although their list was boundless, in the end it became our repertoire!

Shortly, they insisted that we cater their little functions, too! We had no real taste for that aspect of the business (merely wanting to run a little shop), but the rich were autocratic in their mandates. So we entered their alien kitchens, and rode in their demeaning service elevators as we were bidden.

Oddly, the old rich brought us ascendancy and the new rich took it away. The fine old families nurtured our talents until the press and public discovered our skills. And we forever lost our cachet when the first middle-class matron (wanting a toney bar mitzvah) crossed the saffron-colored portal.

Later we were more provident perhaps—though never so chic. And we sold *The Store* long after our original clientele had ferreted out a new, less-establishment caterer as their purely private preserve.

I have never been anything but philosophical about this disaffection. The very rich (and the very social, too) live in a small world that is growing smaller every day. They are an endangered species, and one must forgive them their exclusive diet of passing fancies.

No book about the rich, however, would be complete without one of their favored recipes. The following formula for "Millionaire's Pound Cake" was passed on to me by an inordinately lovely heiress (from Texas, naturally) who thought it rightfully belonged in my repository.

Try it for yourself—it's a mite spendthrifty even for the rich.

MILLIONAIRE'S POUND CAKE

1 pound sweet butter *(room temperature)*
4 cups sugar
6 large eggs
¾ cup milk
4 cups cake flour
1 tablespoon vanilla extract
½ teaspoon almond extract
½ cup lemon juice

1. Whip the butter with 3 cups sugar in an electric mixer until light and creamy. Beat in the eggs, one at a time, mixing well after each addition.
2. Stir in the milk alternatively with the flour until thoroughly blended. Stir in the vanilla and almond extracts. Mix well.
3. Pour the batter into a greased and floured Bundt pan, and bake in a 325 degree oven for about an hour.
4. Combine the remaining cup of sugar with the lemon juice, and heat over a low flame until the sugar is dissolved. Pour over the cake while still warm.

ACKNOWLEDGMENTS

Pity the Poor Rich was written by me, but it could never have been completed without the enormous research and unstinting reportage of Phillip Stephen Schulz (who, besides conducting endless interviews for the project, compiled and wrote all the listings and charts).

A huge undertaking requires huge thanks. It is impossible to acknowledge all the contributions of friends and supporters, but I am particularly beholden to the late writer Ted Burke, as well as to Rosemary Kent, Earl Blackwell, Dr. Robert London, Sue Spitler of Incredible Edibles, Ltd. (Chicago), Dick Kagan of *Town & Country* magazine, Marylin Bender and Charlotte Curtis of the *New York Times,* Arthur Louis of *Fortune* magazine, Ellen Stern of *New York Magazine,* Barbara Knowles of Viking Press, Faye Levine, Bob Mack of The National Council on Alcoholism of New York and Walter Murphy of the National Chapter, and the late Richard Joseph, travel editor of *Esquire* magazine for all their assistance.

I am also indebted to Robert Masello, Anne Marie Cloutier, Luther and Margo Henderson, Marie Timlin, Joe De Rosa, Sophie Nicholas, Bruce and Pati Scott, and Ross Firestone for their invaluable snooping and recounting of "rich trivia."

One grace note: a special thank you to Myra Greene for her generous assistance typing and revising the manuscript at deadline's door.

B. G.

PITY THE POOR RICH

I Who Are They?

(Or . . . What It Takes to Be
Rich These Days!)

The quintessential distinction between the very rich and their less fortunate brethren once was pointedly demonstrated to me by a wise black lady in the service of one of America's top ten families.

Watching me (through half-mast eyes) while I paraded my culinary accomplishments, as an alien caterer, in her vast and gleaming kitchen, she finally opened a near-bare refrigerator, peered inside, and then glanced back at my fanciful arrangements of mousse and terrine.

"Honey," she said at last, "the big difference between *them* and us is that *we* eats better. *All* of the time!"

We, and that is an all-inclusive pronoun for everyone not lucky enough to be well-heeled, probably *sleep* better, too. Unburdened as we are by the besetting social pressures that cause upper-crust cookies to crumble faster.

For one thing, everyone has this misconception of what it takes to be really rich. Or, to put it vulgarly: how much dough is required for big *bread!*

The answer is not so dispiriting as you would imagine. A study of wealth (by *U. S. News & World Report*) revealed that there were over 240,000 people with net assets of a million dollars or more in 1976. Taking inflation and our generally upward-bound standard of living into consideration, some economists predict that this figure will rise by an additional 10,000 (newly minted millionaires) by the end of 1978.

That amounts to 1 out of every 900 Americans, or roughly about one-tenth of 1 percent of the total population.

Are you ready for this?

Of the 250,000 millionaires, 150,000 are a cadre of enterprising strivers who merely acquired a little capital recently and who will have to be considered just *poor rich* unless their fortunes climb drastically. *Middle-class rich* come next: 75,000 plutocrats who have been around somewhat longer and who privately concede to assets in excess of $50,000,000 to $75,000,000; they do not seem as equally an endangered species! The only true

1

"un-knockables" in the bunch, however, are the last 25,000. Members of that elitest group (whose minimum wealth requirement is $200,000,000) are the only ones entitled to be called *really-really rich!*

*　　*　　*

Of the current crop of *poor rich* a few statistics are worth noting: while most of the new moneyed are assumed to be married men (over 40), a goodly number actually appear to be young women (the widows and daughters of those dear departed achievers). As a matter of actual fact, half of all the recent millionaires are female. Their average age is 33, and their average financial worth is about $2.2 million, just a jot lower than the average $2.4 million for (quick) males in the same economic stratum.

The *poor rich* (at first glance) appear to be an uncommonly dull lot. They work extraordinarily hard for their success but are often less inclined to take business risks than the average *poor poor.* Many are loners, but though their politics seem unorthodox and they wear blue jeans all the time, their fundamental attitudes toward money, the work ethic, and aspiration seem about the same as those ascribed to Horatio Alger a hundred years before: "Work hard today and you will be amply rewarded tomorrow!"

Journalist Arthur Louis (of *Fortune* magazine), who has been a rich-watcher for years, claims: "None of the self-made of today seems to be stupid." Just plain lucky!

Notable *poor rich* include such Johnny-come-on-lately millionaires as TV's Johnny Carson, who is so solid these days that Kenneth Tynan wrote: "If someone were to say in print that Johnny takes home around $4 million a year, I doubt whether anyone at NBC would feel an overpowering urge to issue a statement denying it."

Winsome and (it is claimed) unspoiled boy-jockey-millionaire Steve Cauthen is exactly the size mini-folk-hero America loves best. From the time he turned 16, back in 1976, this over-achiever on horseback has ridden 217 *wins,* 187 *places,* and 156 *shows* for a total of some $3 million in prize money (of which he kept 10 percent). Since then, Cauthen has signed advertising contracts to endorse cereals, airlines, men's toiletries, and even *small* cars! In the works is a TV special and a biography to be called *The Kid*, plus a line of Cauthen-inspired posters, T-shirts, bathtowels, and jockey shorts, naturally, which will bring his net earnings to well over the $5 million mark in 1979.

Robert Margolis and Stan Buchthal, both 30, who were roommates at Boston University, claim to have dreamed of money-making schemes since they were kids. After a spate of less-than-toe-hold employment in New York (Madison Avenue ad agencies for Margolis and Seventh Avenue rag businesses for Buchthal), they pooled their communal resources and started a men's wear design firm in a town house furnished with some fine Oriental rugs and Buchthal's pet dog—and very little else. They were a runaway success from the start. Their casual high-school-to-college gear has racked up sales in excess of $12 million a year, and they now have a West Coast operation and a factory in Europe. Buchthal also has a yacht!

A goodly portion of new millionaires' assets appear to be solidly frozen: William Mullis of Georgia (frozen shrimp); Harry Umphrey of Maine (frozen french fries); and unlikely Jeno Paulucci of Minnesota (frozen chop suey). But Peter Frampton's assets, on the other hand, are liquid gold!

It took only one stunning LP to turn this minor rock artist into a multi-conglomerate. His first album, "Frampton Comes Alive!," has sold over 11 million copies in only a year and a half—and transformed a young, attractive Briton into a minor American monetary legend. Frampton's corporate sales for 1977-78 are estimated at $13.2 million—not counting the singer's S.R.O. concert tours, which will surely treble his earnings. And he's barely turned 27!

Colleen McCullough, though a bit longer in the tooth, is not a whit less fiscal a commodity. At 40, Miss McCullough's second novel, *The Thorn Birds,* has been top dog on the best-seller lists for over 44 weeks; and paperback rights to the book recently were bid up to $1.9 million (a bonanza in publishing akin to striking oil in your windowbox!). With her earnings from hardcovers, magazine rights, foreign editions, and TV, the *poor rich* Miss Mc. will take home close to $5 million this year.

As another young millionaire, Douglas Campbell, founder of D.A. Campbell and one of the shakers and movers of large blocks of stock for institutional investors, puts it: "It's getting easier and easier to accumulate a million dollars these days—and the funny thing is, it's going to get even easier!"

Taking a long, hard look at some of the even newer *poor rich* (Muhammad Ali: $5 million a fight; Paul Simon: $2 million a record; Marlon Brando: $2.25 million a movie; and Joe Morgan: $1.5 million a baseball season), it is fairly evident why a mere million has no real status anymore and why, even among titans, there is now a three-class society!

*   *   *

The very names of the *middle-class rich* read like an alphabet soup of the upper strata of society. Start with Aldrich, Auchincloss, Baird, Baker, Biddle, and Burden, and go through to Whitney and Woodward and you have the *Almanach de Gotha* of America's great "endurables." Old family stock for cushion and lots and lots of preferred stock for added clout.

The past few years have been roughest of all on the *middle-class rich* in business. With the ups and downs of a capricious "bearish" stock market, yesterday's seemingly secure millionaire (in the $100 million class) is very likely to wake up and find himself one of today's hundred neediest capitalists (worth less than $20 million).

Think about it—before you laugh!

That is a fast 80 percent decline in net worth. And while not depressing enough to launch a full-scale revival of the famous '29 window-ledge swan dives, it remains a shuddering reality for all the boys who play tycoon.

Case in point: H. Ross Perot, at 48, is a true "has-been billionaire"! The founder and chairman of the board of Electronic Data Systems of Dallas, Perot watched a fluctuating economy dwindle his personal holdings in that company from a peak high of $1.5 billion in 1970 to a less-than-lofty $100 million in 1977. Perot is still in the upper half of the *middle-class rich*, but that hardly makes him special since there is no exclusivity in being a kind of "run-of-the-millionaire."

Between the old and the new *middle-class rich* there are wide disparities in attitudes toward money. Old *middle-class* money (the kind one associates with the cream of America's familial society: Fricks, Houghtons, and Hirshorns) has a golden glow of culture and philanthropy about it that terrifies *nouveau middle-classmen*. Because, frankly, the *arriviste,* though just as rich, doesn't consider himself in that league.

Unlike the robber-baron dynasts who cut and chiseled their way through the nation's early hard rock, the new nabobs usually amass their fortunes from the most prosaic kind of soft goods (such as pet food, nail polish, or frozen citrus juice) and retain something of an inferiority complex about the source of their money.

Oddly enough, in business the old *middle-class rich* are most often found seated as chairmen of a company's board of directors—while their less-seasoned counterparts are the aggressive shakers and movers of its growth. The new *middle-class rich* push the stock forward, but the old *middle-class rich* give it a touch of class!

Leonard N. Stern is a wunderkind of American industry's new *middle-class rich*. A demi-billionaire at 40 (and technically one of the *really-really rich* at this point), he remains stolidly in line with his bootstrap confreres in all attitudes except his startling business vision.

A few years back when Stern was one of the new breed of *middle-class rich* himself, he was quizzed about starting an art collection in the manner of the Rockefellers and du Ponts with some of his pet food money. He replied with a broad wink and the information that he wouldn't *dream* of splurging on the sort of hobby that was accessible to multi-millionaires only.

Recently he was asked the question again. The entrepreneur whom *Fortune* classified as one of the wealthiest businessmen in the world ($500 million to $700 million) shook his head even more firmly.

"I can't see all that money hanging on the walls without earning interest. Besides, pets are my hobby! I am into gerbils now. I have over 20."

Gerbils are his business, too—along with pedigreed dogs and cats, parakeets, rabbits, and tropical fish plus all the myriad accessories necessary for maintaining their health and welfare. And quite a remunerative business it obviously is! Yet 20 years ago when Stern took over his family's flagging Hartz Mountain Bird and Birdseed enterprise, the official opinion of the operation on Wall Street was exactly that: birdseed!

By canny diversification and even cannier real estate manipulation, Leonard Stern consolidated Hartz Mountain into one of the largest privately owned corporations in America. Scarcely shy about his abilities as visionary, Stern explains the rise.

"This was a typical family business. Now it's a professional one. I took Hartz from 60 products to over 1,200 this year . . . from packaging to integrated merchandising and imaginative marketing."

Mr. Stern's homes (a cooperative on Fifth Avenue, a summer house on Long Island, and a condominium in the Caribbean) are all appropriately stocked with pets. Besides the gerbils, there is a miniature schnauzer always in residence. But no Arabian horses, no prize Brahma bulls or Black Angus livestock—the rich man's more accepted prerogatives.

But, then, Mr. Stern never thinks of himself as a rich man. With a candor that is uncommon even in the *middle-class rich,* he avers: "I like my dog. But if you ask me if I like all dogs, the answer is no! I hate the other guy's dog who's always coming around to crap on my lawn."

*　　*　　*

In the old days there were only two kinds of rich: old money and new. And the *nouveaus* were expected to suffer all the slings and arrows of their social betters—precisely because they were so dreadfully gauche. A friend of Charlotte Augusta Astor once wrote her " . . . if you don't rise to the occasion and cut Mrs. Potter Palmer *dead* at a first meeting, the pushy woman will surely have the temerity to invite you to her private spa at Saratoga . . . or, even worse, to sail for Europe on her yacht!"

Those days are gone forever. Today's *middle-class rich* (though busy amassing millions with the same ruthless energy that inspired their forbears) rarely have yachts at all, and private spas are few and far between! Moreover, from all evidence, the *middle-class rich* today maintain an almost vulgar humility about their possessions. Aside from their informally furnished cooperatives and the token foreign car, most of these captains of industry (and their families) live absolutely unadorned lives.

Unashamed to be Spartan, Jack Eckard, 65, the drugstore chain magnate (whose fortune is reputed to hover at about $150 million) bespeaks this mien of the new modesty when he talks about his money.

"The trouble with wealth," Eckard apologized, "is that you can't eat any more than you've *been* eating. And I still want to smoke more than two or three cigarettes a day—but I can't have 'em!"

Another relatively new *middle-class rich* tycoon is Anthony T. Rossi, chairman and founder of Tropicana Products. He made his bundle by squeezing billions and billions of oranges dry in Florida. Rossi's company now sells this fruit juice throughout most of the U.S. in cartons—and exports it (canned or frozen) to 12 foreign countries as well. Last year's crop (though not a banner year for oranges because of bad weather and worse publicity) still brought in revenues in excess of $110 million.

Mr. Rossi, a native of Sicily who still speaks with a heavy Italian accent, takes elaborate pains to point out that his enormous wealth has not materially altered him.

"You've got to watch [out] that money doesn't spoil you. The temptation is there, but by the grace of God I can say that I am not spoiled. If you love money . . . ," Rossi says, "money never satisfies you! The more you have the more you want. I use my money as a tool to be useful—that's when you really find joy."

A Baptist convert, Mr. Rossi's joy obviously is compounded annually by his good works. The best way he can use his money, he believes, is to help spread Christianity—everywhere! He has spent millions to further the work of missionary services and

Bible schools and once even started a branch of the Baptist Church in Sicily, which must rank as one of the more foolhardy gestures of his ecumenical charity.

Less benevolent in his adopted land, Mr. Rossi's company is one of the Florida Citrus Growers who pay Anita Bryant to be their industry spokeswoman. When assailed for his continued support of Miss Bryant (an ardent anti-homosexual fundamentalist), Mr. Rossi replied to his detractors that "he would pray for them."

But Mr. Rossi prays a lot anyway. He also teaches Sunday school at a church in Bradenton, Florida, where he lives.

Among the new *middle-class rich*, Clint Eastwood is the most well-heeled actor still working in films. The movie industry estimates that he receives at least $10 million a film for any part he chooses to play.

"I may very well be the last of the rich performers to show his face to a camera . . . ," Eastwood concedes. "Bob Hope used to be the top-money dog, of course, but he got tired of letting them paste him together. But why pursue the point? Talking about how much money someone has is grotesque."

Like the rest of the *middle-class rich,* Eastwood shares a reticence about discussing his net worth. "We all make do," he says sadly, "with what we have in this world."

The *middle-class rich* ethic is based on two propositions: 1) playing down the size of your wealth; and 2) enriching the community by your donation of good works. In Eastwood's case, his tight-lipped demeanor belies the funding of gymnasium facilities in the slum areas of Los Angeles.

By and large, Eastwood and his crowd are the important endowers, bestowers, and collectors in the U.S., and "The Arts" would be lost without their active support. In society, the same *middle-class rich* are the *laissez faire* vigilantes that marshal every major philanthropic cause and fund-raising event that takes place between Park Avenue and Worth Avenue from October to May.

Consider the letterheads for "The April in Paris Ball," "The Boys' Harbor Fashion Show at Saks Fifth Avenue," or "The Sportsarama Gala for the Performing Arts Center of Saratoga" and you will observe (at the side of the page and well below the emblazonment of honorary chairpersons) a list of discreet, most often italicized names. These are the committee members and sponsors. Inevitably there is a Hilson, Amory, Strawbridge, Whitney, Nicholas, Mortimer, or Pratt among them—and for the very best reason in the world. They are the so-called *platinum* names of all good works. Besides attracting sterling types to an "affair" (as it is inevitably referred to in beneficent backrooms), the *platinum* people are responsible for filling at least 25 tables at any event to which they subscribe. Multiply that amount by the usual $200 a couple, figure 10 couples per table, and you will see just how valuable *middle-class rich* are to the world of charity. Moreover, they never demand any credit for their bounty!

In a recent study of theatrical investors (the backers of Broadway plays, broken down as to income), 70 percent of the major shareholders turned out to be members of the *real* middle class. Another 28 percent were classified as *poor rich* (some a wee bit poorer after a string of flops) and a fractional 2 percent as *middle-class rich*. That should give you some idea of the group's celebrated caution and blandness.

Eccentricity, the *middle-class rich* are said to learn at nanny's knee, is the exclusive preserve of the *poor rich* (who have nothing to lose by being singled out for their privileged quirks) and the *really-really rich,* who have nothing to gain!

"Anyone at all can *make* a pile of money . . . ," noted one member of the *middle-class rich* to another disparagingly, as flashbulbs popped and TV reporters edged microphones forward to interview Nelson Rockefeller on the day he formally announced his bequest (to the vice-presidential mansion) of Max Ernst's $35,000 surrealist "bed." "But it takes a sense of fittingness to know *how, when,* and *where* to give it away!"

* * *

Mr. Rockefeller is obviously one of the *really-really rich* of this country and not always in the good graces of his lessers. But if the super-rich act quirkier on occasion than their fiscal second cousins, it is only a defense mechanism (against the deadening responsibility of their status) and not solely caprice. After all, the richest of the really established billionaires have fortunes so large and diversified that the number of zeros alone could permanently defuse a computer.

Rockefellers, Fords, Hunts, Ahmansons, du Ponts, Mellons, Phippses, Dorrances, Pews, and Motts are just a few of the capitalist families in America whose combined wealth equals all the other small change left in the world.

Forgive them their ducal ways and their patrician penny-pinching because it is their way of life. They are both under-insulated to sensibility and over-protected from criticism. If they never carry cash or credit cards when they shop or dine out, it is not because the idea of ad valorem is precisely demeaning but rather that it is unessential. The *really-really rich* get what they want—without it!

In a neighborhood such as Beverly Hills, where spending vast sums of money impresses no one at all, the shopkeepers of profligate Rodeo Drive recently reported a new standard for really "upfront largesse." Two OPEC princesses (plus body-guards) arrived in L. A. on a Friday afternoon, too late, alas, to make The Bank of America by closing time. Chagrined and loath to hop their private jet back to Saudi Arabia empty-handed, the princesses simply kicked up their Ted Lapidus heels and called a few numbers in Washington and San Diego. In no time, an armored limousine arrived with a bank official bearing alms: $200,000 for the girls' spending spree. And that's how really *rich power* works all over the world. Even Rockefeller and Ford excesses often pale by comparison!

In Texas, Anne Burnett Tandy over-qualifies as one of the *really-really rich*. A middle-aged madcap heiress of parts, with all the assurance and equipage standard to her class and locale (half-million acre spread; four ranches; hundreds of thousands of cattle and quarter-horses; and a spanking new I. M. Pei house), she recently found herself in want of a new jet airplane.

"I wanted it and I knew that I wanted it red," she says, recalling her impact on the intimidated Lear Jet sales force. "I said to the saleman, 'Honey, I want to buy this thing and I don't need a brochure to pick out the color neither. You have the shade of red I want . . . because it's a color you use for the trim on other planes. Now, I don't want a bit of lip from you that you've never done it before because you're gonna do it for me and furthermore . . . [Mrs. Tandy loves to retell this and she laughs at her own punch line] I don't want you to *ever* do it again for *anyone* else! You hear?'"

Highly vocal on the powers of her persuasion about anything she wants in this world, Anne Burnett Tandy stands tall and walks fast. She has to; her Waggoner Ranches in South Texas are the largest tract of privately owned land in the U.S. She is a lady who wears a Stetson hat and 40-carat diamonds at the same time; she is philosophic about the authority of her empire.

"Not everyone has a jillion dollars," she puffs, "and a lot of 'em who do are capons!"

Sitting in her jillion-dollar house in Fort Worth (where she rests up between bouts at "Four G's," one of her Waggoner outposts, or Palm Springs or even Paris), Mrs. Tandy is vocally one of the *really-really rich* who is "all intact." But whether she is so adept at throwing her weight around precisely because she is *so* rich or *so* Texas is a moot point.

Two needlepoint pillows in the Tandy bedroom are emblazoned with her "jillionaire" philosophy:

"The difference between the men and the boys is what they pay for their toys" is a maxim inscribed on one. The other reads even more succinctly: "I'm not the miller's daughter, but I've been through the mill."

Being a "jillionaire" might buy one a few Modiglianis and Lautrecs (Mrs. Tandy's collection is prime), but it no longer guarantees asylum from a hostile and prying world.

Charles Allen, 75, said by Wall Street admirers to be worth $500 million to $1 billion, is a shy and reclusive man who found himself suddenly labeled "a godfather figure . . . who brushed shoulders with persons of financial ill-repute and convicted swindlers" in a disputed *New York Times Magazine* story by Lucian K. Truscott IV, which appeared early in 1978.

Mr. Allen, who rose from a humble boyhood in a cold-water flat on the West Side of Manhattan to become the founder of one of the top ten investment banking houses in the world (with a controlling interest in Columbia Pictures, Seven Arts Productions, and The Grand Bahama Port Authority), was notably bruised by the insinuation and the unwanted publicity, and threatened the newspaper with a $3 million law suit. And though Allen has been involved in at least half a dozen Federal District Court suits that alleged securities fraud of one kind or another, the *New York Times* duly printed a retraction—and reportedly paid Mr. Allen a healthy sum as further balm.

Money cannot sanctify his reputation, of course, but it might defray some of the cost of his lifestyle. Mr. Allen is said to be famous for lunching at the 21 Club and honoring the maitre d' with hundred-dollar bills. He also owns a 1,500-acre estate ranch near Phoenix, Arizona, that, as far as anyone knows, he has never seen.

Times back, a man of parts knew he was financially insulated when the press was afraid to mention his name. But today, as S. Bunker Hunt is so fond of saying, "There are no standards left . . . only brands."

When his father, H. L. Hunt, was going strong, a *really-really rich* person's life was more secure. And a millionaire was able to pursue his pleasure without ever once dipping into his capital. He merely lived on interest—and pretty high on the hog from all accounts, too.

But today, competition among "class conscious" millionaires has made that practice as passé as the piggy bank. Even the richest of the *really-really rich* learn, early on, how to make do on a token pittance so the major portion of their interest can be reinvested and bear bigger and bigger pile-ups (which, of course, eventually just get invested, too!).

If the system seems unfair, think of it this way: the rich might be getting richer, but their standard of living is as lousy as yours and mine.

"Tight money," you hear them murmur, as they have their old minks altered again, for the fourth go-round.

"Sorry. Too expensive! Money is *so* tight," they say, as they shun filet of beef for chicken as the *plat du jour* at their daughter's coming-out parties. "It's simply all because of tight money, darling."

And you had better believe it.

One observation of my own about the rich might be slightly biased. Certainly jaundiced, it comes from a long series of painful interchanges with all three classes of rich at one time or another. Take it from the candid ex-caterer, the *poor rich,* the *middle-class rich,* and the *really-really rich* are blood brothers at one moment of truth: after the ball.

They might have been overcome with delight at every detail of your meticulous craftsmanship—or they might have grumbled and carped about everything you cooked. No matter. In the final analysis, rest assured, they will never (absolutely) *ever* pay the bill on time!

And that, as far as I can detect, is the chief and pertinent link among the monied, everywhere.

II   Where the Big Money Came From
(Or . . . Who's Minding the Story?)

Let us not overpraise the rich (dead or alive)! But it is a sad fact nonetheless that the 1970s have witnessed the demise of four of the richest men ever to have lived in the same century.

Howard Hughes, billionaire, died April 5, 1976.
John Paul Getty, billionaire, died June 5, 1976.
Howard L. Hunt, billionaire, died November 29, 1974.
John D. MacArthur, billionaire, died January 6, 1978.

Together, this quartet (wealthier by far than the collective pharaohs) gave rise to an entirely new category of *really-really rich* and necessitated the adoption of yet another nomenclature to describe it. Thus the term *googolaire* was coined.

Exact definition: highest pecking order—even among a world of superlative peers.

For the uninitiated rich-watchers, *googol* is a loose cognomen for the mathematical phenomenon that occurs when a numeral is followed by a hundred zeros. Ideally, the *googol* occurs in a bank balance, but that's not a prerequisite for understanding the principle.

The *googol* was invented by D. E. Kasner, Professor Emeritus of Mathematics at Columbia University some years back, who explained it in lay terms as: "A quantity more than twice the number of rain drops falling on a city in a century, or twice the number of grains of sand at Coney Island!"

A gracious plenty by any standard even if it turns out to be merely *money*. The aforementioned *googolaires* (Hughes, Getty, Hunt, and MacArthur) had more than money in common, however. Besides being unaccountably well off (one is tempted even to say *filthy* rich when speaking of Hughes), they were all mutually obsessed with remaining unobtrusive. That might either be a character trait necessary for becoming a *googolaire* or a symptom of the condition once you have it!

Hughes never went out (except for a semi-yearly haircut). Getty often wore the same pair of socks for months at a time. Hunt always brown-bagged his lunch. And MacArthur was so

15

inconspicuous that his neighbors thought he was a Social Security pensioner until he died.

If you should assume that such demeanors merely indicated the *googolaire's* advancing senility, have another thought on the subject. Not one of them *ever* owned a yacht. They drove very old cars most of their lives and were accustomed to, or at least seemed to relish, wearing old clothes, which, even if they had been expensive to begin with, were always so rumpled by long usage that the wearers appeared dowdy and shabby.

These men, to borrow a thought from Thomas Wiseman, were not interested in the flamboyant accoutrements of their money at all. They did not fancy its power to affect world events, and they did not savor the sybaritic pleasures it could easily afford them. In most cases they didn't even use their money to corrupt.

They were only interested in money as a purely personal possession—the way lesser men might feel about owning a harem!

For the *googolaire,* a substantial column of numbers on a page is the ultimate satisfaction. In this form alone, money has an abstract beauty and a cleanliness akin to great (non-sexual) love.

To the richest of the *really-really rich* it seems (and so all the psychologists aver) that money fulfills its natural function best when it is unseen—in the dark of a computer's insides, where the shameful act of multiplication can be done unwitnessed. Only the profit printout is a testament to its ever having taken place!

*   *   *

The fiduciary crunch of a *googolaire* such as Howard Hughes was far greater than any conventional reckoning can calculate: roughly, somewhere over $2½ billion. But the estimate pales when it is compared to his towering stockpile of quirks and neurotic crotchets.

Hughes was always called "the Huck Finn of American business," and the pity of his legend is that he outgrew it. A boy wonder who hated book learning and went to the oil fields instead of college, he inherited two gifts from his father: remarkable mechanical wizardry and damn good looks.

The elder Hughes (also a Howard) fresh from Harvard to Texas, developed and patented a new kind of drilling bit for oil prospecting that "chewed through hard rock as if it was Oh Henry bars!" He could have been the first billionaire in the family, but he died young and his 18-year-old son inherited the charge. Studying his father's invention, H. H. II conceived the notion of fabricating the drill bit but leasing it to wildcatters (for a residual on any pay dirt) instead of selling it outright. That way, when a prospector struck it rich, Howard (and the Hughes Tool Co.) struck it even richer.

Shortly, he was able to abandon the oil fields for palmier territories (such as motion pictures and aviation), where Hughes made a real splash. At 22 he became a Hollywood director-producer and gained immortality by "discovering" Jean Harlow.

A decade later, he went into the airline business. Hughes bought a struggling carrier named Transcontinental and Western, reshaped its finances, and renamed it TWA. And that didn't hurt his whiz-kid image, either.

Hughes was undoubtedly an original. He made millions in aviation, but when the aircraft business slumped, he diversified to aerospace hardware and radar. Buying the red-ink R. K. O. Studios during the birth pangs of television, he unloaded it seven years later (when TV already had begun to rattle the film industry) to independent television producers for a whopping million-dollar profit.

He created medical foundations and established charities without even knowing how to spell the names of the diseases they attempted to cure. He bought hotels and gambling casinos in Las Vegas and Nicaragua the way other rich men collected Picassos.

In the last 10 years of his life Hughes's erratic behavior and off-base personality warped his judgment and atrophied his acumen. Instead of financial manipulation, he now turned to old movies for diversion. Holed-up in a womb-like fortress, he watched films from morning until night. Any kind of airplane story was his first choice, but it also is reported that his all-time favorite was *Ice Station Zebra*, an adventure tale of U.S.-Soviet confrontation in the Arctic. Hughes's aides claim he watched that movie at least 150 times—and would recite lines of dialogue aloud (to the screen) as the drama unfolded.

He died of kidney failure and uremic toxins on a hired jet flight between Acapulco and Houston.

From all accounts (and more will be published as the lore sinks in) the boy wonder became a glamorless old man at the end, a hopeless, drug-addicted recluse (terrified of germs) who wallowed in self-neglect and physical debasement. A man who ultimately died without comfort, friends, or a legal will!

Chances are the problems of the Hughes estate (and the continuing battle to claim it) will run well into the next century before it is ever probated.

*   *   *

After Hughes, the richest of the late *googolaires* was definitely John Paul Getty, whose assets were said to be in excess of $2 billion. An inheritor himself, he parlayed his legacy into that astronomical figure by a combination of what has been called "delicate manipulation and foresight," which is a kinder way of putting it than ruthlessness.

When he was still a stripling, young Getty had notions of becoming a career diplomat and spent two years at Oxford preparing for that vocation before his dynast-father turned him firmly in the direction of the family oil fields and bid him breathe deep.

The elder Getty knew that the sweet smell of success was contagious, and his own bankroll had been accrued by some very provident oil leases before his son got the fever.

Young Getty made good at everything he touched. Well, practically. As a wildcatter, he made a million before he was 25. As a tomcatter, he fared less well, however. Married three times in less than six years, Getty always paid out shopping settlements to secure his freedom. A tough fighter, he once took on his own mother in a court battle to gain control of the family business—and won! His mother didn't speak to him for years, but after the proxy struggle, Getty had become sole owner of a prolific empire that not only prospected and drilled for oil but transported and marketed it in service stations worldwide.

An ambivalent sachem, he indulged himself in cultural windfalls and beautiful women. He acquired rare French furniture and even rarer French pornography. (His collection, often said to rival King Farouk's, was mostly acquired from that late, deposed monarch, whom Getty affectionately called "Tubby.") Getty also was a flawless linguist and, besides reciting classic Greek and Latin, could out-talk and out-bargain any German, Frenchman, Spaniard, or Jew—in his own tongue!

Asked how it felt to be a billionaire, Getty said:

"That's a stupid question because there is no such thing. . . . An individual may own a business worth a billion, but little of that is ever available to him in cash. And as for bank accounts, no *smart* man keeps that amount on deposit. He invests it! In business."

Another of Getty's quotes about his money makes a dandy epitaph (noting the failure of his five marriages and subsequent divorces):

"I would gladly give all my millions," he said, "for just one lasting marital success!"

Conceding his defeat in that quarter, at least, after his death, J. P. Getty listed only 12 major legatees in his will. All of them were women; and only one of them was an ex-wife. To compensate for his deficiencies as a husband, Louise Lynch Getty receives $55,000 a year for the rest of her life.

*　　*　　*

Getty's rival for oil supremacy, Howard L. Hunt, was a man of equal pecuniary contrition. If Hunt was shy of being a bona fide billionaire at the time of his death, he was also slightly uneasy about what tide of fortune had helped him to acquire his money. He is reported to have mused often on the arresting possibility of waking up bankrupt, "Just so's I could see if I had the stuff to make it again!"

His 10 children (and step children) had that golden opportunity—and muffed it! When Hunt made out his will (an estate hovering around $999 million), parcels were evenly divided among them *all*—with a codicil stipulating that any one of them who challenged the will would forfeit his rights to all benefits and properties forever.

None did and three of his heirs (N. Bunker Hunt and W. Herbert Hunt—who run the family business—and Lamar Hunt, owner of the Kansas City Chiefs) are said to be well on their way to becoming demi-billionaires already. However, unlike their late father, they keep a low public profile.

The elder Hunt was a vocal, far-out, right-wing absolutist. He was a cracker-barrel philosopher whose multifarious assets helped him found a rash of quasi-totalitarian organizations: Facts Forum, The Life Line Foundation, and Bright Star Foundation. All of these actively preach, publish, and broadcast a Hunt doctrine that is squarely anti-communist, anti-labor, anti-social reform, anti-eastern money (as opposed to Texas money), and anti-liberal at large.

Born in Illinois, Hunt quit school and made his way west when he was a very young boy. Faced with an untamed territory and limitless possibilities to tame it, he turned to trade. He became, in rapid order, an itinerant barber, cowpoke, lumberjack, and gambler and eventually achieved success as an Arkansas cotton grower.

It was cotton's decline in the early twenties (when market prices plummeted and ruined him) that finally set Hunt on his course to becoming one of the richest men in America.

Being a family man by nature, with several mouths to feed, he considered any harebrained scheme that could make him a quick buck for groceries. According to which legend you subscribe, Hunt is reputed to have either borrowed $50 or won it in a card game (he liked to vary the details of his life story from time to time) and invested it in an oil-drilling rig.

Which came up a gusher!

Hunt attributed his great success in the oil business to his gambler's nose: "I can always smell a royal flush," he said. It's a moot point as to whether his olfactory sense alone was responsible, but Hunt did manage to multiply his balance sheets to seven figures by sharp trading in oil leases.

A faddist in most things, Hunt never drove a new car in his life and, as mentioned, always carried his lunch in a brown paper bag. The contents of which, reliable sources state, was always the same: one carton of cottage cheese, three organically grown prunes, and an apple.

* * *

John D. MacArthur, a minister's son from Pittston, Pennsylvania, who started his $1 billion-plus fortune by selling dollar-a-month insurance policies door-to-door, liked to say that his enormous wealth stemmed from bad luck. "Other people's calamities, that is. . . . "

The founder of Banker's Life and Casualty Corporation began his business in 1928 (with borrowed capital from his brother) and saw the investment through the terrible days of the Depression until it finally showed a profit.

"I shot my mouth off to my brother about making a big success, so I couldn't throw the sponge in when things got tough after '29," he recalled years later. "Insurance companies were going out all around me like lights on a Christmas tree, but I was too damn scared to admit failure. . . . So I guess you could say I didn't fail by default."

At one point his assets shrunk to less than $100. But eventually the Depression proved a bonanza as MacArthur's company was able to pick up small policyholders relinquished by other companies that failed. In 1940 the business was valued at $1 million. Thirty-eight years later MacArthur was one of the richest men in the world. And the vast holdings at the time of his death included banks, textile factories, oil wells, and half the real estate in Florida.

"I'm not a builder," MacArthur often said, "just a salvage operator. When somebody gets a tit caught in the wringer, they call me to get it out!"

Homespun to the point of being eccentric, MacArthur enjoyed his "plain-folks" pose as much as he obviously relished making money. Though he was the owner of the Gulf and Western Building and the Lincoln Tower apartment complex in New York, he never went to that city.

"It's too noisy and too high for me," he said. "I'm just a small town boy.

MacArthur drove a beat-up blue Cadillac (a dead giveaway

of the million-plus status), wore drip-dry shirts, and made it a policy never, never to fly first-class on any commercial airline.

"My tail fits very nicely in a tourist seat," he explained. "Besides, I don't think of myself as first-class material."

Oddly enough, MacArthur did not even seem to think of himself as rich.

"The company I work for is stinking rich," he admitted grudgingly on one occasion, "and I just happen to own the company. I certainly didn't have much to start with. I remember my father saying, 'Johnny, don't be a hog. You can be a pig. Pigs get fat but hogs get slaughtered!' "

*   *   *

With the expiration of the four original models for *googolaire,* tycoon-watchers have been casing the pages of *Fortune* and quizzing the big boys on Wall Street for some hints as to their successors. The names of Charles Allen, Edwin Land, and N. Bunker Hunt all have been bandied about from time to time, but the matter was summarily resolved late in January, 1978, when headlines of major newspapers throughout the country proclaimed that: "America's only living 'billionaire,' Daniel Keith Ludwig, was being sued for $10 million by his ex-wife."

The quotes around the word billionaire were obviously intentional. No journalist ever has been able to get close enough to Mr. Ludwig to ask him whether or not the crown fits!

A virtually unpublicized megalo-magnate, D. K. Ludwig is a man who values his privacy more than his money. Like the late Howard Hughes, he shuns all media interest in his activities and his private life. Unlike the eccentric Texan, however, Ludwig's demeanor is so bland and his image so completely unidentified that this superman of finance is able to come and go (like an aging Clark Kent) in almost utter anonymity.

Now over 80, Ludwig may be seen on the streets of New York every morning, from Monday to Friday, pacing himself from his apartment at 785 Fifth Avenue to his office at Burlington House on the Avenue of the Americas (in a skyscraper he coincidentally owns) in half an hour flat.

Few passersby give him a second glance. In somber suit (topped by a plastic raincoat on wet days), Ludwig might be just another elderly Manhattanite on his way to work.

Michigan-born (albeit Texas-raised), this man who amassed worldwide dominion without any boost from family legacies or marital alliances has the bland, chameleon quality of an upper-middle-class business executive rather than a mogul. And he is barely recognized by his employees, no less an uncurious public.

He lunches (often alone) in public restaurants such as "21" or the Warwick Hotel, across the street from his office. At his present age his social schedule is somewhat limited, but he still makes and takes his own phone calls and walks to all of his appointments when he can. In a month of Ludwig-watching, I observed him hail a cab on only two occasions and both times it was snowing.

Like MacArthur, when he travels afield (to one of his overseas outposts), D.K. Ludwig inevitably flies on a commercial airline—always in the economy section. An aide explains: "Mr. L. is interested in neither publicity nor mystery." He just prefers being inconspicuous.

The Ludwig interests are equally unacknowledged. National Bulk Carriers (his main operating company in the U.S.) owns supertankers, petrochemical plants, real estate, farmland, cattle banks, a 4,650-square-mile rain forest empire deep in Brazil's Amazon, and a brace of super-hotels in the Caribbean. (Ironically, during the illness that finally led to his death, Howard Hughes was holed up in a Ludwig hotel, the Acapulco Princess, a dazzling Mexican showplace rumored to have cost over $64 million and solely financed by Ludwig.)

Because he owns all of his enterprises outright—and there are never any stockholders to question his business decisions—Ludwig is virtually a king of industry. But with no heir apparent to whom he can leave his control and no trusted manager being groomed as a successor, Ludwig's empire might not survive his reign.

From the newspaper stories circulating about his private life, no better public image of Ludwig has come to light than the one already known. Even the photographs printed of the man date back 30 years or more.

He has been married twice. The first marriage (to Gladys Madeline Ludwig, who is suing him for $10 million back alimony) broke up almost 40 years ago amid much bitterness. *Time* magazine reports a daughter by that marriage. Ludwig claims he has no heirs.

The second Mrs. Ludwig (Ginger) is said to have a son by a previous marriage. Ludwig never has confirmed any such relationship and is reportedly leaving all of his estate to cancer research (his favorite charity).

The Ludwigs maintain a penthouse in Manhattan and, until a few years ago, had a modest but unremarkable establishment in Darien, as well. After the newspaper stories about Ludwig's private life, a close, Connecticut neighbor was quizzed by the media about what the Ludwigs really were like.

"I can hardly remember," the woman said quite frankly. "They never came out of their house."

No surprise. *Googolaires* are obsessively unobtrusive folk, as I pointed out a while back.

*   *   *

The dearth of *googolaires* in America should not be lamented too loudly. The lone-wolf billionaire might be an endangered species but is not really worthy of conservation. An important thing to remember about his breed is that he rarely shared his good fortune—with stockholders or anyone else!

Most of those *really-really rich* who stand well below the billionaires in American enterprise operate out of public corporations that allow shareholders (as their partners) to rise or fall with them. However (a worm in the apple), a goodly number of the principal investors in these great institutions inevitably turn out to be family members of the founders.

The following list gives a brief idea of *who* is still running *what!*

WALL STREET BRAHMINS

Company Name	Controlling Family
Allen & Company	Allen
Merrill Lynch	Lynch, Merrill, Leness
Bache & Company	Bache
Francis I. du Pont & Company	Du Pont
Goodbody & Company	Goodbody
E.F. Hutton & Company	Hutton, Coleman
Harris, Upham	Harris, Upham
Dean Witter & Company	Witter
Walston & Company	Walston, Fleming
D. A. Campbell	Campbell

FINANCIAL WIZARDS

Banking Firms	Controlling Family
Chase Manhattan	Rockefeller, Champion, Chase
Bank of America	Gianini, Peterson
Morgan Guaranty	Gates
Security First National (L.A.)	Austin
Irving Trust	Murphy, Irving
Mellon National	Mellon, Mayer
Wells Fargo	Cooley
First National of Chicago	Livingston

INDUSTRIAL TITANS*

Corporation	Controlling Family
Exxon	Rockefeller, Harkness, Loeb

*Taken from *Fortune*'s "500 Largest Industrial Corporations" list (1976), in order of importance.

INDUSTRIAL TITANS *Continued*

General Motors	Du Pont, Mott, Sloan, Pratt
Ford Motor Company	Ford
Texaco	Hill, Gates, Norris, Lapham
Mobil Oil	Rockefeller, Nickerson
Standard Oil of California	Rockefeller, Harkness
Gulf Oil	Mellon, Scaife, Brockett
IBM	Watson, Fairchild, Smithers, Hewitt
General Electric	White, Gardner, Borche
Chrysler Corporation	Chrysler, Hannah, Hutton, Mellon
IT&T	Geneen, La Croix, Paine
Standard Oil of Indiana	Rockefeller, Blaustein
Shell Oil	DeGolyer, McCurdy
U.S. Steel	Phipps, Gates, Schwab, Du Pont, Rockefeller, Blough
Atlantic Richfield	Rockefeller, Anderson
E. I. du Pont de Nemours	Du Pont
Continental Oil	Rockefeller, Tarkington, McCollum
Western Electric	Gorman
Proctor & Gamble	Proctor, Gamble, Cunningham
Tenneco	Symond
Union Carbide	Acheson, Kenan, Mason
Westinghouse Electric	Westinghouse, Mellon
Goodyear Tire Company	Rosenwald, Goodyear, DeYoung
Phillips Petroleum	Du Pont, Phillips
Dow Chemical	Dow
Occidental Petroleum	Hammer, Gimbel
International Harvester	Deering, McCormick, Bercher
Eastman Kodak	Eastman, Philipps, Clark, Carter

Sun Oil	Pew
RCA	Sarnoff, Rockefeller
Bethlehem Steel	Mellon, Grace, Rockefeller
Rockwell International	Rockwell, Atwood, Ramos
General Foods	Hutton, Davies, Post, Woodward, Igleheart
Firestone Tire & Rubber	Firestone, Woodworth
Amerada Hess	Hess, the British government
W. R. Grace	Grace, Phipps

REAL ESTATE TYCOONS

Lords of the Land	Kingdoms
Daniel K. Ludwig	South America, worldwide
The Rockefellers	Rockefeller Center
Laurance Rockefeller	The Carribean
The Weyerhaeusers (TACOMA)	Northwest timberland
The Irvines	Irvine Ranch
The Klebergs	King Ranch
The Schines	All those hotels
The Wiens and Helmsleys	Empire State Building and others
The Corrigans	Shopping centers, apartments
The Phippses	Palm Beach, Miami
The Cohens and Arlens	New York office buildings
Robert David Lion Gardiner	Gardiner's Island, Long Island
The Astors	New York slum areas

III What's Happened to Society?
(Or . . . Is Clout Alive and Well Anywhere?)

"It isn't what it *used* to be . . . " is a statement the rich seem to make about everything these days. Gone are the times of great stone mansions on Fifth Avenue and legendary 60-room cottages at Newport. East Hampton (once an exclusive and restricted bastion) is now filled with dress manufacturers, and Park Avenue is filled with office buildings! Yesterday's 12-course dinner parties are usually brunches today—more often than not, eaten on the hoof and inevitably served by hired hands.

The old order changes with small things. Kingdoms fall and rulers are deposed. Gloria Vanderbilt becomes a blouse designer, and the Dodge mansion is razed to make way for 2-bedroom studio apartments. While none of this is momentous, it presages the end of gracious living for some. Even "The Ball," once an established social event, is slip-sliding away into oblivion; and its descendant, "The Public Charity Event"—crammed with quasi-movie stars and deduction-happy donors who come to see rather than be seen—is, alas, no substitute.

Like everything else that the rich are into these days, even their soirees are commercial ventures.

But no matter how bad it looks at the moment, the social swim is not exactly landlocked, merely becalmed. And coming-out parties like polo matches are still definitely agenda items on the calendars of the right people in the right centers of the U.S. Social Establishment. Which are (for the non-cognoscenti): New York, Philadelphia, Boston, and San Francisco—in that stripe of importance.

Not everyone agrees. In Philadelphia, for instance, the pecking order is: Philadelphia, New York, and Boston. In Boston, it's *only* Boston! In San Francisco the lines of demarcation are: West Coast versus East Coast, with the western division way out on top.

Aside from geopolitics, "Society" is essentially a game of names; and money (though hardly a social debit) is not a prerequisite for being a player. The names that count most in "Society" are a group I choose to call the "Clout Crowd." The

29

monikers of this collection of elite, ostensibly East-Coast person-
alities appear with amazing frequency in the society columns of
Eugenia Sheppard and Suzy Knickerbocker, and their comings
and goings are regularly reported in either *Women's Wear Daily,*
the "People" section of *Time* magazine, or "Notes on People" in
the *New York Times.*

An additional measure of clout is also determined by a full-
page photograph and/or story in the pages of *Town & Country*
magazine (the last outpost of pure social chronicling left in the
United States).

Clout Crowd names are of such interest even in the
hinterlands that editors often devise ways of sneaking them into
local features. In her "People Watching" column of the *Detroit
News,* Eleanor Breitmeyer writes essentially home-town gossip—
but if she chooses to report that Mrs. J. Anthony Forstmann
(Charlotte Ford, a local girl) was seen discoing at Manhattan's
Studio 54 recently, she inevitably adds the fact that C-Z Guest,
Maggie Newhouse, and the Duchess d'Uzes were all "hustling"
nearby.

Ironically, in Eugenia Sheppard's syndicated column,
"Around the Town," the Clout Crowd names are always set in a
slightly bolder typeface than the rest of the text—so that even at
a distance, nearsighted readers may observe that:

> **Mrs. Charles (Norma) Dana** is Chairman of the Feather Ball this
> year. Her committee of busy bees who will help raise money for
> Just One Break, Inc., includes **Chessy Raynor, Phyllis Wagner,
> Nan Kempner,** and **Pat Mosbacher.**

The Clout Crowd members who are listed below are
probably the weightiest because they represent established family
position as opposed to mere social celebrity. They are here rated
(as in a *Michelin Guide*) for their newsworthiness in the assorted
media over a period of a single month in-season.

The constituents of the Clout Crowd with a *Social Register*
pedigree have been compiled, along with their social lessers (or
in some cases betters) who have lost that official sanction for
some personal malfeasance or a matrimonial blunder. The
difference in status will be noted by a lower case "s.r." after the
designee's name.

Media	Symbol
Eugenia Sheppard column.	*
Suzy Knickerbocker Column.	*
A mention in both Eugenia's and Suzy's columns during the same period.	**
Women's Wear Daily.	
Mention in the "Eye" column.	WW
A feature story, with or without photographs.	WW1
Time.	
Mention in the "People" section.*	T
New York Times.	
Mention in "Notes on People" column.	NYT
Mention in a feature story in "Family/Style" section.	NYT1
Town & Country.	
A photograph in "Parties" section.	TC
A feature story or a full-page fashion photograph.	TC1
Miscellaneous society columns outside New York. A story mention or listing at a social function.	+

Time's "People" section is not to be confused with its literary offshoot, *People* magazine. *People* has declassed itself as an arbiter of the social world in this listing by its apparent editorial social ambivalence. While the Clout Crowd is often seen in the magazine, their appearances take second place to *People*'s interest in the activities of rock stars, transsexuals, and other assorted crazies! In a sense, a listing in *People*, therefore, represents a minus for any solid social figure.

THIS IS THE CLOUT CROWD

Mrs. Richard Adler **

Mrs. Harcourt Amory **, NYT, TC, s.r.

Mrs. Muffie Amory **, WW, TC, s.r.

Mr. & Mrs. H. Loy Anderson **, TC

Mrs. Brooke Astor **, WW, NYT, TC, TCx, s.r.

Mr. and Mrs. William Astor *, s.r.

Mr. & Mrs. Louis Auchincloss **, NYT, TC1, s.r.

Mr. & Mrs. Nicholas Biddle **, WW, TC, s.r.

Mr. & Mrs. Alfred Bloomingdale *, TC

Miss Cele Briscoe **, WW, T, NYT

Mr. & Mrs. William F. Buckley, Jr. **, WW, WW1, T, NYT, NYT1, TC, s.r.

Ms. Amanda Burden **, WW, WW1, T, NYT, TC, +

Mr. Carter Burden **, WW, NYT, TC

Mr. & Mrs. William Burden **, NYT, TC, s.r.

Mrs. Henry Byers **, TC

Mr. Truman Capote **, WW, WW1, T, NYT, NYT1, TC, TC, TC1, +

Mrs. Gloria (Vanderbilt) Cooper **, WW, WW1, T, NYT, NYT1, TC, TC1, +

Mrs. Gardner Cowles **, WW, TC

Mrs. Frederick Ames Cushing *

Mr. & Mrs. Charles Dana, Jr. **, TC, s.r.

Mrs. John Drexel III **, WW, TC, s.r.

Mrs. John Drexel IV *

Mr. & Mrs. Angier Biddle Duke **, WW, TC, s.r.

Ms. Doris Duke **, WW, NYT, TC

Mr. & Mrs. Irenee du Pont TC1, s.r.

Duchess d'Uzes (Peggy Bedford) **, WW, WW1, T, NYT, TC, s.r.

Mrs. Charles Englehard **, WW, TC

Mr. & Mrs. Ahmet Ertegun (Mica) **, WW, WW1, T, NYT1, TC, TC1

Mr. & Mrs. Marshall Field V *, TC, s.r.

Mrs. William Fine **, T, NYT, TC

Mr. Henry Ford II **, WW, NY, NYT1, TC1, +

Mrs. Christina Ford **, WW, WW1, NYT, TC, +

Mrs. J. Anthony Forstmann (Charlotte Ford) **, WW, WW1, NYT, NYT1, TC, TC1, +

Mrs. Arthur Gardner **, TC, +, s.r.

Mrs. Ira Haupt **, TC

Mrs. J. H. Heinz II **, WW, TC

Mrs. Deane Johnson (Anne McDonnell Ford) **, WW, WW1, T, TC1

Mrs. Lady Bird Johnson *, TC, s.r.

Mrs. Rose Kennedy **, WW, NYT, TC, TC1, +

Mrs. John Kempner (Nan) **, WW, NYT, T, TC, TC1, +, s.r.

Mrs. Walter J. Laird, Jr. (du Pont) *, TC1, +, s.r.

Mr. & Mrs. Alfons Landa **, TC1, +

Mrs. Albert D. Lasker (Mary) **, WW, WW1, T, NYT, TC, TC1

Mrs. Joseph Lauder (Estee) **, WW, WW1, NYT, TC, TC1, +

Mrs. Arthur Levitt, Jr. **, TC, +

Miss Anne Lindsay **, WW, T, NYT, s.r.

Mrs. Gerald Livingston TC1, s.r.

Mr. & Mrs. Goodhue Livingston, Jr. **, TC1, s.r.

Mr. & Mrs. Jock McLean (Brownie) **, WW, NYT, TC, TC1

Mr. & Mrs. Frank McMahon *, TC

Mr. & Mrs. Algur H. Meadows **, WW, T, TC, s.r.

Mrs. Joseph Meehan **, WW, TC, s.r.

Mr. Jay Mellon *, s.r.

Mrs. Lewis Gouverneur Morris **, TC1, s.r.

Mrs. Emil Mosbacher **, TC, TC1

Mrs. John Mosler **, WW, TC, TC1

Mrs. John D. Murchison **, TC, +

Mrs. Clyde Newhouse (Maggie) **, WW, NYT, NYT1, TC, TC1, +

Mrs. George Ohrstrom **, TC, s.r.

Mrs. Jacqueline Onassis **, WW, WW1, T, NYT, NYT1, TC, TC1, +, s.r.

Mrs. William Paley (Babe) **, W, WW1, T, TC, TC1, +

Mrs. Claiborne Pell *, WW, T, NYT, TC1, s.r.

Mrs. Dallas Pell **, WW, T, NYT, s.r.

Mrs. Thomas Phipps **, WW, TC, TC1

Mr. & Mrs. John S. Pillsbury, Jr, *, TC, +, s.r.

Mrs. Arthur Pratt **, WW, NYT, TC, s.r.

Mrs. Chessy Raynor **, WW, WW1, T, NYT1, TC, TC1

Mr. & Mrs. Nelson Rockefeller **, WW, NYT, NYT1, TC, +, s.r.

Mrs. John Roosevelt *, TC1, s.r.

Mrs. Laddie Sanford (Mary) **, WW, WW1, T, NYT, TC, TC1

Mrs. H. Donald Sills **, WW, TC1, s.r.

Miss Cornelia Livingston Van Rensselaer Strong **, WW, T, NYT, TC1, s.r.

Mrs. Bertrand Taylor III **, TC

Ms. Anne Ford Uzielli **, WW, WW1, NYT, TC, TC1, +

Mr. & Mrs. James Van Alen **, T, TC1, s.r.

Ms. Jean Vanderbilt **, TC

Mr. Phillip Van Rensselaer *, TC1, s.r.

Mr. Stephen Van Rensselaer, Jr. **, WW, T, TC1, s.r.

Ms. Diane von Furstenberg **, WW, WW1, NYT, NYT1, TC, TC1, +

Mrs. Diana Vreeland **, WW, WW1, NYT, NYT1, TC, TC1, +, s.r.

Mrs. Cornelius Vanderbilt Whitney **, WW, NYT1, TC, TC1, s.r.

Mrs. Robert Wagner (Phyllis) **, WW, NYT, TC

Miss Heather Whitney **, WW, T, NYT, s.r.

Mrs. Robert Winthrop *, TC, s.r.

Mrs. William Woodward **, WW, T, NYT, TC, TC1, s.r.

Mrs. Oscar Wyatt **, WW, TC

"Either one's life is attractive or it isn't," Diana Vreeland stated authoritatively a while back. Mrs. Vreeland was not speaking of the Clout Crowd when she said it. Because, as everyone knows, CCs all lead perfectly *beautiful* lives.

Of course what passes for beauty in New York is usually pooh-poohed in the rest of the country as "absolute exhibitionism."

New York Society

New York Society is the least ingrown of all the tribal institutions in this country where heredity still counts for something. "Precisely because there are a lot of different strata of New York society," states Charlotte Curtis, associate editor of the *New York Times,* "it's easy to crash."

Another New York society observer, Rosemary Kent, corroborates her opinion.

"Look at the art crowd or the music crowd. They're absolutely starving for new faces at their dinner parties. They'll take up with anyone if he's truly talented. Even weirdos . . . and I am not speaking of Andy's crowd either!"

She points out that "the sports crowd adores to mix with the jocks and name-drop that Dave deBusschere is spending the weekend at 'the valley.' And the theater crowd—all those Park Avenue groupies! Don't ask where Liza would be without them. Where would they be without her?"

Both ladies agree that there are five separate levels of rarefied strata where the Clout Crowd seems to operate: art, music, sports, the theater, and the easiest one to crash, the charity ball scene.

"That's because there are so many of them," says Rosemary Kent. "It's a whole lot harder to crash society in a town like Columbus, Ohio, or Indianapolis or Dallas, where there is only one!" Miss Curtis concurs.

At the top of the heap in New York (transcending any categorizing) there is still the blue-blood aristocracy that has no concern whatsoever about newcomers crashing their ranks. They are the names of legend and lore: the Livingstons, Van Rensselaers, Pells, Morrises, Winthrops, and Roosevelts.

Not the richest families by any means, they are the ones with the most impeccable weight to their heirloom sterling. For the most part, the members of this pure, patrician enclave eschew the circus aspect of their social position. They all have clout, but they maintain very private lives. They have been prominent on the island of Manhattan for a long, long time.

They know it. Their friends know it. And they "damn well couldn't care less who else knows it!"

Possibly because of its geographic position, New York society generally is accepted as a cultural hurricane that churns up "The Arts" in this country with seasonal regularity. But at the eye of the storm, it seems there is always a Rockefeller.

At the moment, the Rockefellers finance ballet (the New York City Ballet Company and the Eliot Feld Ballet); theater (a $50,000 grant to New York's Circle in the Square); museums (Abby Rockefeller founded the Museum of Modern Art and her daughter-in-law, Blanchette, is now its president. Rockefellers are also weighty contributors to the Museum of Primitive Art, the Metropolitan Museum of Art, the Whitney Museum, the Museum of the City of New York, and the Cooper Hewitt Museum.) No wonder David Keiser, the director of Lincoln Center, remarked recently:

"How remarkable of the Good Lord to reincarnate the Medicis intact—and just change their surname to Rockefeller."

Most so-called "different levels" of New York society imbricate. And those who belong to one exclusive corps (such as the museum elite or the horsey set) manage to survive transplanting into another, such as the yachting crowd or the opera circle, easily. But one stratum of New York society where a Rockefeller has yet to shine is the world of fashion.

The Clout Crowd is intensely fashion conscious and always has been. News reports of their comings and goings are as much embroidered with elaborate descriptions of what they are wearing as with whom they are *seen*. And thus it has been since the days of Miss Godey's book.

In the seventies, however, the CC's fashion consciousness has been raised to include their favored couturiers as bona fide companions. And the labels most likely to appear on a "most wanted list" to flush out a little informal dinner for the Shah of Iran's sister or to lend flash to the "Mandarin Ball" are those belonging to the very "in" designers who make the social swim, swish!

Geoffrey Beene, Bill Blass, Donald Brooks, Stephen Burrows, Calvin Klein, Arnold Scaasi, Giorgio St. Angelo, Pauline

Trigere, Diane von Furstenberg, and Valentino are names dropped with such stunning regularity in Suzy's and Eugenia's columns of late that the uninitiated easily could mistake them for bluer bloods. Singly, they sell dresses, boutique items, cosmetics, and even home furnishings on occasion. Together, their power is plenipotentiary. When they were all seen (albeit individually) at a new restaurant within a week's time, reservations quadrupled. It became impossible to get a table to dine there for at least a month afterward. The quality of the service almost instantly declined, and the food was a disaster, but no one seemed to care. Most of the patrons who followed the fashion leaders were all established CC denizens who *never* question the arbiters of taste!

One supreme CC authority, whose fashionable dicta the rest of the pack await with a reverence usually associated with a sermon from the mount, is Halston.

Roy Halston Frowick, wearing his opaque, mirrored sunglasses, sitting in his mirrored office at United Nations Plaza, with orchids growing in mirrored pots on his mirrored desk, calls all the shots for the beautiful people. His advice about what to serve and whom to invite for a dinner party is valued almost as much as his counsel about which of the Halstons a hostess should buy for the occasion.

Probably the most important tastemaker in the world, this 46-year-old millionaire, born in Des Moines, Iowa, and raised in Indiana, has created such an aura about himself that he receives more weekly fan mail than Robert Redford. He also is mentioned twice as often in the daily press.

A Halston dress is such a status security blanket (even for the Clout Crowd) that his Wheeldex of formidable clients reads like a blue book; Muffie Amory, Brooke Astor, Lily Auchincloss, Amanda Burden, Rocky Converse, Jane Dudley, Doris Duke, Nan Kempner, Mary Lasker, Jaqueline Onassis, the late Babe Paley, Marie-Helene de Rothschild, and Diana Vreeland, to name only a few!

Halston's favorite expression for all of his friends and customers among the CC's is "Sweeticakes." But though the sweeticakes wear his beautiful creations at all the beautiful places from one end of the U.S. to the other, Halston never travels. His single trip to L.A. occurred a few years ago when Elizabeth Taylor literally "seduced him over the telephone" into designing a dress for her to wear to the Academy Awards.

"But Liz is royalty, and you have to obey her every command," he apologizes reluctantly.

Most often, Halston hangs around his town house or his mirrored office, being paid court to rather than courting.

"I get very bored when I leave New York," he says. "Everyone everywhere else looks somehow dowdy!"

While the rest of the country is willing to write off that rebuff (painful as it might be) as mere East Coast snobbery, Philadelphia is not concerned in the least. But then the Main Line is always two years behind the rest of the U.S. in everything and proud of it.

Philadelphia Society

Dogma among Main Liners (where family aristocracy still abounds) holds that the function of the genteel is preservation of proper deportment. If it sounds academic, it is. "A territorial finishing school" is what Alison Vanderbilt called Philadelphia society. "It's still not even co-ed!"

The most astonishing aspect of the place is its air of conversion. Not unlike a Mennonite sect downstate, Main Liners catechize their toehold on all existing institutions. If a newcomer from another part of Philadelphia (or another part of the country, for that matter) manages to move into their territory, they must either adapt or evacuate. Fast!

Arrivistes in short order dress like the Main Line, talk like the Main Line, and think like the Main Line! And they paranoiacally assume (like the Main Line) that the rest of the country's social milieu is patterning its norm after theirs! During the "Blackout of 1977" two Philadelphians stranded in New York went to the Gotham Hotel Bar for a quick drink before attempting to bed down for the night. Served iceless martinis, they were absolutely delighted. That's how they drink them in Bala-Cynwyd.

Curiously enough, a good deal of the Old Guard elsewhere (in Wilmington and Pittsburgh, for example) *is* impressed with Philadelphia's dowdy standards and attempts to emulate the *écru éclat* of the Main Line dowagers. But not New York.

The Clout Crowd views Philadelphia's rigid caste system (no Catholics, no Jews, no theater types, and no gays to speak of unless their names are Cadwalader, Chew, or Ingersoll) as provincial and pretentious. And they find the "low key" atmosphere of the Main Line either mildly ludicrous or downright depressing—depending upon which member of the Crowd you are quizzing.

On the other hand, Philadelphia society sees the CC as "too fast, too fancy, too showy, and much, much too disorganized."

Old Guard Bostonians tend to share the opinion.

Boston Society

Boston society is a different excursion from Philadelphia's rigid sodality although both cities share a common, mutual air of rectitude. Mrs. Liddon Pennock, a younger member of the Main Line, is very vocal about the contrast.

"Oh, my dear. Boston is ghastly," she says. "In Boston you simply do not get enough to eat," which turns out to be a fairly common visitor's complaint. A young Englishman who was staying with the Homans a few winters back during the debutante season, reported that he was so hungry all the time, he devised a series of late-evening constitutionals for himself. On the pretext of a long walk to the Charles, he would drop in at the Ritz for a sandwich or two before retiring.

Quite possibly this Spartan conceit of prandial undernourishment in Boston was started by the late Mrs. Jack Gardner. A legend in the early part of the century, Mrs. Jack, as she was called (but never to her face), was something of a non-conformist.

In ascetic Boston, where everyone else was measured by a low street number on their Beacon Hill town houses (the best adjudged to be precisely between Louisburg Square and Charles Street), Mrs. Jack had two mansions—back-to-back—in the highest section of the Hill.

She also made it a point to have more horses, more coaches, more automobiles, more servants, more feathers, and, none too discreetly it is said, more love affairs. She governed despotically over dinner parties, and hers were the most lavish in the city.

When her husband died, unexpectedly impoverished, Mrs. Jack gave up the high life entirely. She sold off everything. Purchasing cheap marshland in the Fenway section, she built a "final home and monument" far from Boston proper. When guests came there anticipating the usual Gardner fare, they found themselves settling for clear broth and a single lamb chop. Mrs. Jack had retrenched; the first of her class to turn penury modish.

Her frugal hospitality swept Boston society, which has never quite recovered from its thrall. Nowadays (mainly due to Julia Child's diligence and local sway) dinners are a wee bit more effulgent, but the nickname of "Austerityville" still clings to Boston society—like morning fog off the Charles.

Detractors claim stringency is practiced because social Bostonians are not as wealthy as their counterparts in New York or Philadelphia. While that might be true to some extent, it seems to this observer, at least, that Spartan personality rather than financial crease determines the size of the portions!

Boston prides itself on being proper. One of Stephen Birmingham's tales underscores its sobriety. When one of the Adams clan was visited by a rather well-known Western beldam, the lady was served a cocktail before dinner. She finished her drink and after a discreet time when no refill seemed imminent, held up the empty glass to her hostess.

"My dear, we have a saying in San Francisco. 'You can't fly on one wing,'" she said. To which old Mrs. Adams calmly replied, "In Boston we *fly* on one wing."

San Francisco Society

The "baby" of the great social hubs can only claim four family names that can be measured against the Eastern aristocracy. And, though there is not a member of the Clout Crowd among them, these solid Californians carry unmistakable weight anywhere. They are: the Crockers, the Hopkinses, the Huntingtons, and the Stanfords. All are of reputation durable and lineage long.

Liberal-minded West-Coasters are inclined to add a few slightly newer surnames such as Fair, Flood, Folger, Henderson, Mackay, Metcalf, Nickels, O'Brian, and Spreckels to this conceit of quadrified S.F. society. But conservatives steadfastly stick with the original four.

West of the Pecos, to have a box at the opera in San Francisco (on Tuesday night only) used to be the unimpeachable evidence of a man's status. And "Horseshoe Circle," looped together by mysterious but invulnerable barriers of society, resisted all the efforts of eager newcomers who tried to crash it—no matter how much gold they laid on the line.

Year after year, the same gilded names appeared on the 14-carat tabs affixed to every seat—and the tenure of a box was generally so prized that it was passed down to a man's heirs as a blue-ribbon asset in his will.

To be a member of the Opera Crowd was to be part of a world of culture and refinements and proof positive that a San Franciscan family had left its rag-taggle antecedents of prospectors and procurers far, far behind.

Today, the turnover in opera boxes has hit the city like a second earthquake.

"I don't care to prove that my name is Folger by putting on a black tie every week," said one long-haired legatee last winter. "Because all that stuff really doesn't matter."

Of the 132 listed boxholders in the late 1960s, less than 83 families still retain them. The opera is not going broke, it's merely going without its golden coterie.

"Society is not dead out here," says Niven Busch, writer/social registree who watches over San Francisco hierarchy like a jaundiced hawk. "It's merely quiescent. Young San Franciscan women refuse to make Cotillion debuts, and young males of the Establishment are in perfect agreement. They prefer jeans to couture and lend the family's Tuesday-night opera box to someone who dropped in from out of town. Usually some New

Yorker! But that's how things go. Change, the French say . . . all is change!" In society, too!

* * *

An unvariable for society is the two lower-case initials that indicate capital status: "s.r.," equalling accepted Establishment in the *Social Register*.

This volume, issued yearly and revised biannually, might not be the only guide to social acceptance in the U.S., but it is one publication that maintains such a decorous air of endorsement about its listings that inclusion becomes an imperative for both jet setters and lesser local squirearchy.

The formidable black and red bible (8¾" square) is published by the Social Register Association, 381 Park Avenue South, in decidedly less-than-grand surroundings. There, in a dusty office, separated by opaque glass and wood partitions and adorned with unframed bird prints attached to the walls with tape and thumbtacks, the Better People are selected by an advisory committee that convenes early each summer to make the momentous decision of who will and who will not make the latest edition.

Utter secrecy surrounds the entire ritual.

A telephone call placed to the Register office met with a refusal to comment on the rumor that the 1979 edition would consolidate the listings of the 10 most important American cities into one volume.

"I am sorry, sir." The secretary at the *Social Register* offices maintains a toneless resonance to her voice and has obviously been coached to a degree of reticence that would do credit to the Soviet embassy. "I cannot make a statement on that subject at this time," she said.

"Will you say who edits the *Register*, then?"

"I am sorry."

"Or how many people make up the advisory board?"

"No." Then an inordinately long pause. "I am sorry, but the *Social Register* prefers not to answer any questions of that nature," she says before the telephone is disengaged.

Through less circumspect shareholders (yes, the *Social*

Register is a corporation), it was adduced later that 1) there had been a consolidation; 2) there are 10 to 12 persons on the selecting committee—and though their number is not always constant, they are the established masters of all social arbitration.

The chairman's identity is heavily veiled, but hearsay gives the editor's role to Dr. Robert Beekman of New York, whose family received partial control of the publication when Louis Keller, the founding father, died in 1922.

The *Social Register*'s thickness is said to reflect the economic state of the country; in boom times it swells, and during a recession it resembles a slim volume of poetry. This year it is enormous!

A marginal note imprinted on the salmon-mousse-colored endpapers bears this cavil:

"If the married name you are seeking has escaped your memory and you can recall the maiden name, reference to the Married Maidens section will then indicate the present name. Consult January *Dilatory Domiciles* for most recent changes."

The *Social Register* is published for profit, and it pays for itself—depending, of course, on its listees' willingness to be included and its hefty subscription rates for support. Price: $35 a copy, with *Dilatory Domiciles* and *The Summer Social Register* $7 per issue.

While many of the Clout Crowd decry the weight of a *Register* listing, most fill in the necessary annual forms the week or even the day on which they arrive.

It might be "just a third telephone book," as C-Z Guest is said to refer to it, but there are damn few "wrong numbers" inside. Even its new, enlarged format is trenchant. A board member explained *(sub rosa)* that the editions were now consolidated because cities such as Boston, Philadelphia, and New York were no longer isolated *ententes cordiale.*

"The aim of the book," she went on to explain, "is not to drop people who defect socially but rather to list those who, in our changing world, are a constant!"

That the *Social Register* is arbitrary in matters of morality cannot be denied. Divorced persons (forget how exalted they are socially) are excised from its pages if the details of their rupture become too public or too ignoble. But divorcees often are restored to its good graces when, as in the case of Nelson Rockefeller, they become Veeps.

The *Register* also will (without explanation) list persons of no background or social position whatsoever merely because of an association with public office.

Thus, James E. Carter (Jimmy) is endowed with not only **, WW, WW1, T, NYT, NYT1, TC, TC1, and +++ in this book but also carries a neat little "s.r." after his name, too!

IV Where They Live!

(Or . . . What Keeps the Rich at Home?)

In 1962 when the *New York Times* and some other prestigious newspapers across the country announced that Shaker Heights (a verdant if somewhat over-manicured suburb of Cleveland) was *the richest community* per capita in the U.S. according to the Census Bureau report, this town of 36,000 was literally overrun by "confidence men." Investment research firms and municipal bond analysts blossomed overnight at every major shopping plaza. And mutual fund sellers (all wearing Gucci loafers and carrying attaché cases to match) proliferated like worm holes after a good Ohio rain.

There was a mass influx, so great, in fact, that local police had to be called out just to keep the thousands of itinerant salesmen (peddling everything from *Forbes* magazine to Maximillian fun furs) from actually lining up on residents' door steps.

It took a very long time to get the town back to normal, and some wary Clevelanders suggest that it never has been the same. So it is understandable that the Shaker Heights citizenry held its collective breath when the 1970 census figures were about to be released a decade later.

It turned out to be a purely groundless concern, however, for in the last analysis all such classified information was discreetly excised from the census news releases. And though a canny con man might well have read between the lines, since the report succinctly stated that incomes in most established upper-class sections of the country were $10,000 a year higher than the decade before, Shaker Heights never again felt the invasion of those fiscal Fancy Dans!

The unheralded 1972 census dropped Ohio's elitest community to fifteenth place among those rich towns in America with populations of 10,000 to 50,000 residents, but it also contained some territorial surprises for hardy observers of just where the moneyed hang their hats.

The five richest towns in America in the order of their richness, as of this red-hot report, are:

Bloomfield Hills, Michigan
Kings Point, New York
Mission Hills, Kansas
Brookville, New York
Sands Point, New York

All of these towns have something more than high income in common. They are hangovers from an era of early suburban colonization, when rich people lived as though they were *really-really rich*. All established around the close of World War I, when automobile production was in its first flower, these communities represent society's first migration away from cities. And though one is hard put to see the evidence now, they were mainly an attempt at gentlemanly farming. As a matter of actual fact, routinely cruising along Split Rock Drive in Kings Point, a sharp-eyed observer still can spy (cheek-by-jowl with the clutch of $300,000-plus Georgian mansions that line the road) a few weather-beaten farmsteads and one in particular with a notice on its barn siding that discreetly proclaims: "Fresh Milk Sold Here."

Long Island towns such as Sands Point set the style for rich communities all over the country from Bloomfield to Beverly Hills. These enclaves, mossy-lawned and landscaped to a fare-thee-well with magnolia, rhododendron, and dogwood to blend with the natural habitat, are mostly built on lots rather than extensive acreage. Everyone seems to enjoy close confinement with his peers and back-to-back tennis courts in most of these gilded colonies. There are exceptions, of course. Bloomfield Hills, Michigan, is one-acre zoned, but, as one Detroit socialite matron observed recently: "They feel terrible out there if they don't have four or five!" And Brookville, New York (there are three of them: Brookville proper, Upper Brookville, and Old Brookville), is still horse-breeding country—and fairly spacious. As one of the residents puts it: "Fearful of forfeiting our baronial way of life, Brookvilleites still maintain the look of landed gentry—but God knows for how long!"

While most of the Long Island towns are not top-listed among the richest communities in the country, land at Brookville costs approximately double that of corresponding property in the Midwest (for instance, Kansas City's lush suburb, Mission Hills).

Bloomfield Hills is listed first in order of wealth because the median income in that town is $46,715 yearly. Kings Point is second ranked at $40,971. Income in the Mission Hills community averages about $40,707. So you can plainly see there is not much contest of financial clout. The next two areas, however, drop radically as to median income level. Brookville, Long Island (because of its less dense population, although residents in the area such as the Winston Guests keep it prime), rates at only $35,630, and its sister community, Sands Point, comes in at only $35,562—or a full $11,000 below Bloomfield Hills.

These incomes might not appear startling in themselves until you realize that the figure given is for *each* person in the household. If there is a family of five (plus two servants) living in the average Bloomfield Hills home these days, the aggregate income for that ménage ranges about $327,005—which is pretty high living no matter how you slice it.

Bloomfield Hills

This wooded eminence, forty-five minutes from downtown Detroit, probably has the deepest concentration of working rich outside of Leningrad's Pushkin (where the major ballet stars of the U.S.S.R. live). Bloomfield is far less tradition-bound, however. A five-mile-square municipality that has gradually supplanted Grosse Pointe as the purlieu of Michigan's sedate autocracy (no pun intended) for the past twenty years, Bloomfield is now the chief Commuting Stop for all of the auto industry's ranking executives. The roster of families living in the area reads like an *Almanach de Gotha* of the nation's big wheels and includes presidents and ex-presidents of the four major companies, names such as Lee Iacocca, Ford; Lynn Townsend, Chrysler; James M. Roche, General Motors; and Roy Abernathy, American Motors. Bloomfield's social hierarchy, however, is in a state of constant flux, with deed titles shifting after every board meeting—and the state of heated swimming pools and indoor tennis courts often depends upon the fate of a new car model.

Residents hardly ever stay for more than two generations; the young leave for school early and usually don't return. Consequently, as the wife of an ex-president of Ford complained recently, "Detroit's social crawlers never hang around long enough to metamorphose into butterflies!"

Grosse Pointe is still the bastion of Michigan's elite society—and Bloomfielders know it. *They* compensate for longevity and tradition in other ways. Their lives are freer and decidedly more private. Most Grosse Pointe houses are huddled together, and everyone knows everyone else's business. In Bloomfield the homes might not be as formidable but the grounds are twice as spacious.

A pair of Bloomfield young marrieds, attached to GM by family, are proud of their rolling landscape and the small forest that protects them from the road.

"So many trees condition the way of life here," they say. "People know less about each other. In Grosse Pointe the Hudsons know the very day of the week that the Kanzlers have their car washed, and if the chauffeur doesn't get around to it, it's reported along the grapevine!"

"But then," amends the pretty young wife, thoughtfully, "Grosse Pointe is all gossip and play, you know. Bloomfield Hills society, on the other hand, revolves around work!"

It is related that even at parties the conversation is always shop talk in Bloomfield.

"Husbands talk about their jobs, and the wives talk about their husbands. Mainly about how they pushed them into those jobs in the first place," says another of the Bloomfield Hills hostesses.

According to Mrs. Semon Knudsen, wife of the retired Ford president, the cocktail party's five commandments are: "Stand up! Talk! Sip your drink! Don't get drunk! Go home early!" But even Mrs. Knudsen admits that social life is auto-oriented. "I go to General Motors parties and to Chrysler parties—and they come to mine. We're in a competitive business, but we still go to each other's parties. Except for American Motors, of course."

Even in worldlier Grosse Pointe, American Motors is regarded as slightly déclassé by Big Three officials, but that fact is never discussed. While they drink a lot harder at the summit, they never seem to talk about business at all. As a matter of fact, Bloomfielders say the denizens of Grosse Pointe never seem to talk about anything. "They're as ingrown as toenails," says Robert Cadwallader, one of Bloomfield Hills's genuine Social Registerites.

The *Detroit News* holds the view that Grosse Pointe, rather than being insular, is merely anti-controversial—about everything! Issues are tabled the moment they are brought into a conversation, and for proper G.P.s, such burning questions as Gay Rights, Women's Lib, and The Right to Life are moot subjects (" . . . that take place in the East or West, thank God, but never here!").

Grosse Pointe is not exactly 100 percent conservative—one may even find a few Jewish families woven into the social fabric—but it is a far, far cry from the radical-chic society of Bloomfield, where Jews and blacks have been accepted, certainly as good neighbors if not as co-equals. Hills residents are quick to point out this tradition of liberalism. After all, some fine old black families such as the MacNeals, Muthlebs, and Riggses have been living *quietly* on their turf for years.

One social aspect of Bloomfield Hills that is not as democratic is the Junior League. Not everyone can get in! One young debutante who went skinny-dipping (at her own home pool) with a bunch of co-ed school chums was excluded automatically. Another solid gold GM heiress who had her body painted as a New Year's Eve prank a while back when it was considered O.K. to be outré has remained blackballed ever since.

Observers claim these lapses in taste are a product of the transience that Bloomfield Hills residents share.

"The older generation just doesn't stick around long enough to pass on the little refinements of upper-class breeding," says one social arbiter, sadly. "In Grosse Pointe, you see, they inherited their money. Here in Bloomfield we have to earn ours!"

Kings Point

Rolling hillsides, hidden drives, miniature "No Trespassing" markers discreetly affixed to the trees, and endless wooded country lanes marked by prudent banknote green street signs proclaiming first the roadway's name and then, as an after-thought to the uninitiated, in smaller type the legend: "Kings Point, N. Y."

This is Gatsby-land revisited. Millionaire's Row is undefiled, except for the stray ranch house that is obviously in the $350,000 price range and, while not uniform to the landscape, clearly not an eyesore.

But it is those gray stone mansions (once occupied by Astors, Vanderbilts, and Mellons), set back from the road by copse and bosk and still protected by private police who scan the newcomers to their territory like radar beams, that attest to the staggering wealth of the area. Everywhere one goes in Kings Point the warning is clear: "Flashy Spenders Stay Out!"

Kings Point, a village within North Hempstead on the beige Sound-side of Long Island, was incorporated in 1924. It was, early on, a haven for rich New York exurbanites who wanted to raise their families (along with some home-grown tomatoes) in bucolic surroundings far from the madding crowd at the Marguery and the Ritz.

That's all changed now. The lush greenhouses were the first to go when the larger estates were subdivided—and magnates (such as Alfred P. Sloan, Jr., of United Motors and all the Bloomingdales, Chryslers, and Statlers) either moved back to Manhattan or pressed on to more exclusive preserves in Oyster Bay and Locust Valley, due east.

Today, Kings Point is merely a commuter's hop away from the Eastside Midtown Tunnel entrance: a half-hour's drive by car and only slightly longer by the antique North Shore division of the Long Island Railroad. The area is still prime (albeit less than 100 percent WASP in population). These days, Adlers, Beckers, Cohens, and Kauffmans share the elegant terraces and wrought iron grilles of the neighboring Williamses, Ohrstroms, Wards, and Belmonts.

Some tales of Kings Point's past glory are now practically legendary. One choice anecdote concerns Mrs. Dorothy Killiam, who always entertained lavishly at "The Point" whenever she returned from Palm Beach in the late spring. Parties numbering up to two hundred guests were not uncommon events at Mrs. Killiam's estate, but since the North Shore weather was erratic (particularly in May), she always took the precaution of duplicate table settings (both indoors and out) for all of her fetes. If the weather turned nasty, all outdoor furnishings (napery, china, gilt chairs, and bamboo garden tables) were hastily carried into Mrs. Killiam's lawn gazebo—and the guests were none the wiser. If, on the other hand, the sun shone, Mrs. Killiam would merely place a call to the Kings Point Merchant Marine Academy and request a hundred or so young officers (in dress uniform, of course) to dine at her home that evening. The young men usually ate within the house and acted as escorts for the bevy of debutantes that always studded Mrs. Killiam's parties, afterward.

Kings Point society never actively disapproved of this social mix, "because," as Mrs. George Baker claimed after one such occasion, "Dorothy is so damned, lovably democratic."

The Merchant Marine Academy no longer receives such sudden social calls, but the institution still bounds the village, facing Manhasset Bay to the northeast and Little Neck Bay to the northwest. There are few street lights in Kings Point and no sidewalks. At night the streets are barely visible, so students rarely leave the Academy by foot. Even if they did, there is no place for them to go. Kings Point is an absolutely residential community with no cocktail lounges, movies, luncheonettes, or even gas stations permitted within the incorporated village itself. A stranger to the territory must know exactly where he is going—even by car—or face a helpless maze of winding roads and hostile residents. Homeowners will grudgingly give directions, but all of the estates usually are shuttered. No happy throng of laughing sojourners is ever seen on the spacious lawns and tended drives—winter or summer.

All of Kings Point's correspondence with the outside world (for instance, North Hempstead) is conducted by telephone. And all services, such as those of the dry cleaner, the butcher, and the florist, are performed by home delivery, circumspect vans pulling up at the service drive first before being waved into the kitchen entranceway.

Those who still own property in Kings Point hold it dearly (the market price for acreage is still very, very high), and those seeking to acquire entry into the golden community are usually willing to pay any premium for the privilege.

The principal problem that Kings Point residents face, according to Anita O. Nidel, the Village Clerk, is that of noise pollution: snow blowers in the winter and lawn mowers in the summer!

For the past few seasons, residents have been made uneasy by the increase of duck hunters (moving in blinds from the Port Washington area), but the town board has come down hard against these unauthorized sportsmen because Kings Pointers are very conservation-minded. Proliferating indoor/outdoor tennis courts also have been a hazard of late (particularly on one-structure-zoned acreage), but that problem seems to have been arrested since the Village passed an ordinance in September, 1977, limiting the use of balloon covers and dimaxion domes forever.

Crime in Kings Point is negligible. Domestic squabbles are usually the main reason for calls to the police. Burglaries do take place from time to time, but since the installation of a central village alarm system (that ties in with the residents' personal burglar alarms), they have decreased dramatically.

Frank Hartz, the Kings Point Chief of Police, was born in the town and has worked within a five-mile area for most of his life. He lives in an apartment above the Village Hall on Steppingstone Lane, and he is vocal in his praise of the community:

"It's a good place to live. Clean and pretty . . . and I guess it's always going to stay that way. Residents here are very proud of their town. See how well-groomed everything is, how well-maintained. That's town pride!"

A young and wealthy resident of the community, Kim Eichelbaum, 21, of Steamboat Road, completely disagrees.

"That's show business! Don't kid yourself. Everything here

is show. Clothes! Houses! Cars! People in Kings Point have more money invested in their cars than in the bank!"

Mission Hills

It might be only half an hour's drive from Kansas City, but the residents of this pampered and plush-lined community never accept the fact that they live anywhere other than "just down the road apiece from Crown Center."

Distance discourages them so they ignore it completely. Denizens of this suburb—whether they dwell in fake Georgian manor houses on Mission Drive (a winding stripe of silver macadam walled with centennial oaks as far as the eye can see) or in one of the pink stucco "Midwestern" chateaux that dot Sagamore Hills—are always on their way *to* or *from* K.C.

And, unlike the Bloomfield crowd or even the Kings Point commuters, these 4,315 inhabitants of Johnson County are actually the city's "Social Establishment."

Kansas City grew up late: not until the 1890s were fortunes first made there. But the hog barons, the grain princes, and the donut tycoons (such as Armour, Cudahy, and Harvey) soon got culture's call and pressed upward and onward to Chicago. Today, the verdant terraces of Mission Hills are populated with millionaires (in tennis whites sipping Stolichnaya martinis) whose fortunes were made within living memory. Their money might not have the patina of age, but Mr. and Mrs. Donald Hall (President of Hallmark Cards and heir to founder Joyce C. Hall's vision that "it pays to give *the very best*"), the Louis Wards (Russell Stover candies), and the Richard B. Fowlers (President of the *Kansas City Star*) are truly the Clout Crowd across the wide Missouri.

A showy titan of the "Terrace Set" is Ewing Kauffman, 61. A genuine Horatio Alger type, Kauffman rose from pharmaceutical salesman with the dispiriting southwest territory in 1945 to President of Marion Laboratories today. His company is one of the largest drug manufacturers in the country, and his net worth is conservatively estimated at over $150 million.

Kauffman and his wife, Marion, live in a half-million dollar red brick "Feudal" atop one of the winding hills of the colony. He swims nightly in an Olympic-sized pool that is kept at exactly 76 degrees year round, as are the cabanas surrounding the pool. The Kauffmans have a ballroom in their basement (Lester Lanin's band played there) and a fountain with an hour-long cycle of lights, music, and flashing water in the grand style of *Son et lumière* at Versailles. One feature of Kauffman's house that cannot be missed by the silver Cadillacs and bronze Lincoln Continentals that pass below his drive are the twin, towering flagpoles at either end of the patio, which fly the standards of the United States and Canada (for the birthplace of Mrs. Kauffman) whenever the owners are in residence.

"Who in Europe, or in America for that matter," André Maurois once wrote, "knows that Kansas City is one of the loveliest cities on earth?" Well, obviously the Kempers do. R. (for Rufus) Crosby Kemper and his brother, James, both leading Mission "Hillers," are the undisputed leaders of K.C.'s financial, social, and cultural life, and they have been prime movers in the city's endless beautification plans. Earlier, the Kemper family helped settle the issue of whether the city should be named Possum Trot or The Town of Kansas back in 1893. Reason prevailed then and the Kempers have no reason to believe things have changed a jot in the interim. Kemper pride (and funds, of course) has helped establish the Performing Arts Center, the "Nelson Gallery" (actually the William Rockhill Nelson and Mary Atkins Museum of Fine Arts), with the best collection of modern and post-impressionist paintings to be found north of Houston, and Commerce Tower, a landmark of stunning urban redevelopment that preceded Crown Center as a major tourist attraction by almost a decade.

The area of Mission Hills where the Kempers live consists of only 2.1 square miles. The homes in that sector sell from $90,000 to $1 million, with the greatest selection of property in the $250,000 price range. Actually, there is very little real estate turnover in this community since "Hillers" are notoriously settled types.

There are no churches in the actual town of Mission Hills

although there are houses of worship of every denomination, including synagogues, in surrounding villages.

Similarly, there is no shopping area. And while most "Hillers" are car-borne types who think nothing of running downtown to Crown Center twice a day for their necessities, a fair share of socialites meet at the glamor-plus Country Club Plaza to shop in the shadow of a phony Spanish mission replete with eleventh-century minarets.

Every "Hiller" goes to Crown Center at least once a week, however, ostensibly to *do* the Farmer's Market or to *check out* Hall's. Hall's is a mega-specialty store (similar to Bergdorf's and Bloomingdale's combined), where one generally finds Mrs. Bryant Barnes, President of the Junior League, or Mrs. Burnham Hockaday, founder of The Debutante Assembly, selecting Bill Blass or Calvin Klein coordinated sheets and pillowcases for their Mission Hills residences.

Hall's is sometimes referred to in Mission Hills as, "Our fourth Country Club," the other three being those *grandee* establishments that ring Mission Drive and are listed in the *Social Guide* under "Amusements."

Of these, Indian Hills Country Club is the most popular with the younger set, and Peter Duchin vies with Peter Frampton for their allegiance. The Indian Hills pool is said to be slightly larger than those of the other Clubs, but that is unchecked at this writing.

The Kansas City Club is very posh. It definitely has the best golf course and also, according to Lamar Hunt, owner of the Kansas City Chiefs, employs the best bartender in town. Though how he would know is anyone's guess since Mr. Hunt's drink is exclusively bourbon and branch.

The Mission Hills Country Club is the oldest and the place to see the Wards, Fowlers, and McGreevys at play. The Mission Hills Club is rumored to serve the best food, and certainly it has the most impressive wine list.

A little anecdote concerning the authority of the Mission Hills Country Club would not be inappropriate here. Several years back, when Richard Burton appeared in New York in

Equus after a long absence from the stage, a friend and I went to see the play. Afterward, and in a state of elation, we determined to treat ourselves to a great steak. Our choice of dining places was unanimous—a very private (almost clubby) hostelry that is one disreputable flight above the even more disreputable theater district neighboring Eighth Avenue and Forth-fifth Street, Frankie and Johnny's by name.

At this restaurant (steaks and chops only), the food is unparalleled and, though the prices are high, aficionados beat a path to the door. Around the narrowish room at any given time are almost always the great and near-great of the theater and publishing worlds, all of whom are affectionately greeted by the owners before they are crammed together in the dining area.

On the occasion of the *Equus* opening, the restaurant was more than usually crowded, and an attractive young couple seated nearby could not help but notice the theater playbill on our table. They asked about the play and, as Frankie and Johnny's is a close encounter at best, this came as no surprise. I had made other "short-term" friends there in the past.

Reassured of Burton's majesty in the leading part, they confided that they, too, had tickets for the next day's matinee and then proceeded to enumerate their week's itinerary of play-going.

"We do this once a year," the young wife soon divulged. "We treat ourselves to a show splurge in New York."

Where had they come from, I inquired. And Kansas City was the unabashed reply.

"Kansas City?" I thundered over the din, utterly dumb-struck at how two very attractive (if square) out-of-towners had found their way to a cognoscenti lair such as Frankie and Johnny's (still unknown territory to three-quarters of my New York acquaintances). "How in the world did you ever get to *this* place for dinner?"

"Oh," I was assured, "everyone back home knows all about Frankie and Johnny's."

"You find these things out from the guys who hang out at the Club," the young husband interjected, smiling rather smugly.

"That's one of the perks of joining—after tennis and handball, of course!"

Of course. The place: Mission Hills Country Club, Mission Drive, Kansas.

Brookville

Brookville is one golden triad (2.5 miles) with a sense of humor about itself. Mrs. William Bancroft (of Old Brookville) who was Sarah Sturges—and is a viable *Social Register* entry either way—is very funny on the subject of her town's status.

"This used to be 'in-ville' too!" Mrs. Bancroft is reported to have told a visitor from the Middlebury hunt country in Virginia. "But first we lost our foxes. They're an endangered species because of the Long Island Expressway, you know. Then we lost our Mellons, Wards, and Liz Whitney Tippet. They weren't ever precisely endangered—but they moved on, anyway!"

The three Brookvilles (Upper, Old, and plain) used to be heavily into horse breeding and stud farms; and famous flat-racers flourished on most of the region's elegant estates. Instead of claiming that "George Washington once slept here," most Brookville residents point with pride to some rolling meadow or corral where the great racer Man O' War is said to have serviced some willing mare back in the forties.

Today, Brookville's only industry is its millionaires. County officials and local bankers estimate that between 60 and 100 millionaires own all the lavish realty from Hoaglands Lane to Wolver Hollow Lane. These residents are not only elitist, they are fairly invisible as well. They decline listings in the telephone book and *Social Guide* and, zealous to the point of paranoia about their privacy, keep their estate's driveways virtually unmarked.

Brookville (all three towns comprise the incorporated village) is a community fearful of forfeiting any more of its landed gentry to the suburban developments that blighted the rest of Long Island after the close of World War II. Taxes, while fairly stable, are also classically high. The only properties that ever come up for sale are those prodigious *small* Georgian estates ("Marble entrance foyer. Six bedroom suites plus servants' quarters. Oak-paneled library. 25 × 28 step-down living room. Fireplaces in every room, etc.") set on multi-acred parcels that range upward in price from $525,000 to $1 million.

As Mr. and Mrs. Thomas L. Higginson (Upper Brookville) confide:

"What we all want . . . is to maintain as low a profile as possible for the community. To keep Brookville *out* of the public grasp."

The private graspers (all the right people, of course) still do hang out in Brookville no matter how hard the tides of fortune have buffeted their family capital from time to time. Patterson, Thomas, Ward, Cox, and Woods are all names certainly not unfamiliar to society-watchers, and their tribes' doings are duly reported in the local press on occasion. But none of these mint "upper stratosphere" families would ever consider consorting with or, heaven forbid, inviting the likes of Suzy, Eugenia Sheppard, or Rex Reed to their dinner parties or local social functions: like the Dog Show.

"I am sure they are very charming people who certainly seem to work hard for a living," an elderly Brookville *grande dame* allowed. "But if they consider coming to the three Bs to make a mark, forget it!"

What the three Brookvilles have in common is a sense of standard. Everyone takes their role in the community quite seriously. Ardent conservationists abound everywhere, and beautification programs often consist of replacing hundreds of trees and shrubs to keep the area wooded and verdant as it once was.

"Keep Brookville Green" is a cry that sets quite elderly matrons onto the road in their chauffeur-driven cars just to pick up stray *Coke* cans between the wild lupin in the spring.

Any proposed alteration in zoning attracts almost every town resident to the Village Hall, where the hue and cry (and invariably negative vote) opposes all physical changes that community planners outline for the community's "progress."

Animal mania is also a Brookville way of life. And while

complaints of unleashed dogs running at large are supposed to be referred to the Police Warden, any number of prize golden retrievers and dalmations wander the country roads in utter safety because Brookville residents drive carefully on their home turf to safeguard them.

Proper Brookville parents expect their heirs (by the time they reach maturity) to ride well, know good horseflesh from bad, dance acceptably (the *ultra-restricted* Piping Rock Country Club is just down the road in Locust Valley), and, most important of all, to be kind to pedigreed dogs. Girls are expected only to be able to ride. Finishing school takes care of everything else.

Sands Point

This incorporated village within the area known as Port Washington is 66 years old but still remains as gilt-edged and shiny as a municipal bond.

Only 20 miles east of New York's prestigious Sutton Place, this village is twice as rich, three times less populated, and 100 percent better protected.

Set on a lofty peninsula that juts into Long Island Sound, the patrician community does not even maintain street lamps to light a stranger's way to the territory. But then strangers are not particularly welcomed there.

Sands Point is a suzerainty of stately mansions barricaded by wrought iron grilles, with vigilant guards to check a visitor's identity at every port of entry. Aware of its regal antecedents, Astors, Vanderbilts, and Belmonts, the current upper-class citizenry, Johnsons, Porters, Bennetts, and Cohens, tend to treat their town as a less-than-democratic duchy. There are no stores, cinemas, or gourmet dining spots in Sands Point, and there never will be, according to the Village Clerk, who reports that the Town Board annually turns down over a hundred requests for zoning variances.

Public schools, churches, and sanitoriums are similarly banned, but that is not to say that the area is completely unblemished. Twenty years ago, unflappable Sands Point homeowners had two squabbles with the Supreme Court—and after losing both cases, inherited a private school and a synagogue along their shores.

Lately there has been talk of going back to court again (by certain unhappy taxpayers) to disenfranchise the Sands Point Police Force—a disputatious squadron of 19 auxiliary officers that costs the village half a million dollars a year in upkeep.

"And worth every penny of it, too!" says one occupant of a graystone baronial, facing the duck bluffs of Manhas Bay. "This is why one moves to a *safe* community," he continued. "I have 30 rooms in my house, all filled with some very valuable antiques . . . English silver . . . baccarat up the ass! And I want the kind of protection one can't have if the police station is over 5 miles away!"

Oddly enough, Sands Point is absolutely crime-free—and had been for a very long time before the innovation of private patrols.

Newcomers to the community, specifically those in the less expensive ($150,000 to $200,000) ranch houses on the periphery of the grand neighborhoods, have taken a violent stand against the excessive cost of private protection, particularly when other villages in the area (such as Brookville and Oyster Bay) depend solely on town police.

The "Issue" went as far as a referendum on election day, but the Old Guard weathered out the storm.

"If you're living in an early Tudor chateau worth half a million bucks, who's going to complain about a *thou* a year for security?" shrugged one Harbor Road resident. "Worst comes to worst, we simply outrank them!"

Over two-thirds of the registered voters proved him right, and a proposal, on the ballot, to phase out the use of mercenaries was soundly defeated. So, while the men in blue are busied mainly with traffic violations or checking out the homes of families off to Key Biscayne for the winter, most everyone from Middle Neck Road to Shore Wood Drive claims he sleeps better for the victory!

Sands Point's first brush with liberalism occurred in the early '50s when Mrs. Marie Fetsch bought baroque Elm Court

on the Sound and, against overwhelming odds, attempted to
turn the 40-room Luckenbach mansion into a school for gifted
children.

As the community had never permitted a hospital or a
church within its confines, the idea of a school was anathema—
and a building permit was flatly denied.

Sands Point town fathers disclaimed any lack of democracy
in their decision. Reasons were based on hard-line economics
alone, they said.

"A responsibility to keep property values up requires the
preservation of the landscape against the invasion of foreign
institutions."

While the tone of their refusal seemed eminently final, Mrs.
Fetsch did not give up. And wary "Pointers" soon learned to
their horror that the proposed Country Day School plans were
not only advancing but that students were being selected, with
I.Q. standards rated at the "genius level."

Panic overtook the community, and, though no burnings in
effigy took place on the Luckenbach lawns, a genteel flow of
instructive mail suggested in no uncertain terms that the school
remove itself to Great Neck or Port Washington, where the
climate would be less frosty. Actually, public sentiment became
so vocal at one point that Ross I. Dixon, the school's first
Headmaster, characterized Sands Point as a "haven of intellectual bigots."

Mrs. J. Denniston Lyon was so enraged at his charge that
she promptly put her house up for sale as a kennel (even though
residential zoning restrictions forbade such a possibility), an-
nouncing that "since the Point was going to the dogs . . . " she
would be the first to profit by it.

A legal attempt to disestablish the Country Day School was
eventually defeated although it did manage to bring to public
record the fact that the rich—no doubt due to their cloistered
early life—have lower noise thresholds than other classes. An
incredible number of wealthy neighbors of Elm Court testified in
court that they suffered excessively from any cacophony (like the
sound of gifted children's voices).

Out of communal concern, Country Day School had most

of its upper floors sound-proofed. So when Beethoven or Bach is played during school hours, no one on the lee-side of the premises ever hears a disturbing sonata or fugue in the middle of a croquet game.

The only other social crisis in the community of Sands Point occurred when a Jewish synagogue bought The Chimmneys, a 31-acre estate formerly the home of Christian R. Holmes and originally built at a cost of over $2 million.

The Chimmneys was once the prettiest manor house on any Long Island greensward: 42 rooms, including 14 bedrooms and 12 baths; indoor and outdoor swimming pools and tennis courts; and a spacious greenhouse where rare orchids were raised. After the Holmes's deaths in 1941, the estate had been leased as a "recreation center" for the crew of the Free-French battleship, *Richelieu*. Though that fact never sat particularly well with the S.P. citizenry, France *was* technically an ally at the time. In 1945 The Chimmneys was donated to the U.S. Merchant Marine (as a convalescent home), but the government decided it couldn't afford the upkeep!

Actually, no one could afford it, so eventually it became available on the depressed real estate market for one-tenth of the original price. Even so, it was still no bargain when it was acquired by a floating congregation of conservative Jews in the area as a house of worship.

Before the synagogue group could take title to the property, however, an aroused Town Board quickly amended its zoning laws to restrict the maintenance of a church of any denomination on hitherto residential premises.

Cries of anti-Semitism were bandied about as this decision was appealed and rejected, but racial discrimination *alone* seemed unlikely since the Mayor of Sands Point, and a firm voice on the Board, was of Jewish origin himself.

While the case was in litigation, Sands Point became the unwelcome focal point of the entire Eastern Establishment. Then Governor Averill Harriman, a solid "Pointer" himself, called the zoning restriction "un-American, undemocratic, and depressing," even though the best old Jewish families in the community, such as the Bernard Baruchs and the Guggenheims, refused to comment publicly and privately disassociated themselves from the proposed synagogue.

Actually, Sands Point was one rich town on Long Island where there had never been any instance of prejudice whatsoever; it was also the only community in the country where a large number of successful intermarriages were a public fact.

The issue of the Sands Point Synagogue, to put it bluntly, was once again the fear of change. Noise, traffic, parking problems, and loss of privacy were considerably dearer to Sands Pointers' hearts than any "freedoms" one could mention.

When the Supreme Court overturned the Town Board's decision, there was very little acrimony in residents' hearts. Earlier, there had been talk of building walls around the synagogue and planting trees on the roadside to insure its isolation from the community. But little came of these notions. Most Sands Pointers just got around the problem by booking in at the Piping Rock Club on Friday nights and all the High Holy Days!

*   *   *

A listing of the other *richest* villages, towns, and cities follows, with some rude jolts, I should think, for prognosticators of *where* the loot in this country really is buried!

Villages (Less than 10,000 people)	Median Income
Bloomfield Hills, Michigan	$46,715
Kings Point, New York	40,971
Mission Hills, Kansas	40,707
Brookville, New York	35,630
Sands Point, New York	35,562
Great Neck Estates, New York	35,491
Kenilworth, Illinois	34,573
Lake Success, New York	33,952
Hillsborough, California	33,765
Grosse Pointe Shores, Michigan	32,565
Frontenac, Missouri	32,000
Fox Chapel, Pennsylvania	31,074
Indian Hills, Ohio	30,015

Towns (10-50,000 people)	Median Income
Scarsdale, New York	$33,886
Ladue, Missouri	32,274
Glencoe, Illinois	29,565
San Marino, California	25,103
New Canaan, Connecticut	23,889
Palos Verdes Estates, California	23,760
Beverly Hills, Michigan	22,909
Darien, Connecticut	22,172
Highland Park, Texas	21,271
North Potomac, Maryland	21,020
Chevy Chase, Maryland	20,977
McLean, Virginia	20,791
Beverly Hills, California	20,434
Deerfield, Illinois	20,050
Shaker Heights, Ohio	19,928

Medium-sized Cities (50,000-plus people)	Median Income
Bethesda, Maryland	$16,618
Arlington Heights, Illinois	15,686
Bellevue, Washington	14,114
Overland Park, Kansas	13,184
Dearborn Heights, Michigan	12,768
Kettering, Ohio	12,409
Bloomington, Minnesota	12,241
West Covina, California	12,180
Florissant, Missouri	11,944
Huntington Beach, California	11,845
Parma, Ohio	11,618
Lakewood, Colorado	11,336
Newton, Massachusetts	11,157
Garland, Texas	10,876
Clifton, New Jersey	10,754
Cleveland Heights, Ohio	10,683
Irving, Texas	10,600
Mesquite, Texas	10,539
Yonkers, New York	10,462

Major Cities (500,000-plus people)	Median Income
Milwaukee, Wisconsin	$ 9,458
Minneapolis-St. Paul, Minnesota	9,428
Las Vegas, Nevada	9,195
Indianapolis, Indiana	8,859
Tulsa, Oklahoma	8,231
Houston, Texas	8,056
Omaha, Nebraska	8,018
Dallas, Texas	7,984
Chicago, Illinois	7,983
Detroit, Michigan	7,944
Albuquerque, New Mexico	7,737
New York City, New York	7,679
Los Angeles, California	7,511
Seattle, Washington	7,433
Philadelphia, Pennsylvania	7,206
Cleveland, Ohio	7,129
San Francisco, California	6,765
Cincinnati, Ohio	6,411
Newark, New Jersey	6,191
St. Louis, Missouri	5,998
Boston, Massachusetts	5,921

Though the Census Bureau low rates New York as twelfth ranking of all the rich cities in America, more of the *really-really rich* live there than anywhere else in the U.S. (More of the *really-really poor* live there, too! Which brings the ratings *down*—as they say in the television game.)

But since we have been talking of the Clout Crowd, it might be interesting to point out *who* lives *where* in the Clout City. The very best addresses in New York are always the showier rich who are willing to pay a hefty price for eternally polished brass entranceways and sober (well-starched) doormen who hold out an umbrella every time it rains!

Cooperative apartments are considered more chic than town houses in New York these days because the Clout Crowd is into open spaces. The right people all live in enormously airy rooms with terraces (and floor-to-ceiling window walls) facing nothing but open sky. And the merest rumor that another high-rise is contemplated in the neighborhood can cause a downward plummet in the price of freeholds.

Since "pads" like this generally start at a quarter of a million (not including a yearly maintenance fee well over five figures), rumors like that usually are groundless. For, as one managing agent of a new Tower Building preemptorily put it:

"If you can afford to live here, you automatically have the 'blue sky rights' written into the deed!"

Some of the Clout Crowd live at the following "Power Houses" of New York (from time to time at least):

1115 Fifth Avenue
Considered "too far uptown" to be really chic, its residents include such notables as Mr. & Mrs. John DuBois, Mrs. Iphigene Sulzberger, Mrs. George Brewer, and Mrs. Sheffield Anwyl.

1040 Fifth Avenue
Like 1115, 1040 would be casually dismissed except that Mrs. Jacqueline Onassis and Mr. & Mrs. McGeorge Bundy live there.

960 Fifth Avenue
Where Mrs. Charles Shipman Payson paid $900,000 for the Mellon Bruce apartment, and where the Douglas Dillons, the Winthrop Aldriches, the "Jock" McCleans, and Mrs. Henry Parish II all live snugly together.

880 Fifth Avenue
The home of Mrs. William McConnell Guggenheim Gerhard Broadhurst.

834 Fifth Avenue
Mr. & Mrs. Lawrence Rockefeller, Mr. & Mrs. Cornelius Vanderbilt Whitney, Mr. & Mrs. Watson Blair, and Thomas Milbank pay about $6,000 a month maintenance to live here.

825 Fifth Avenue
For those who like smaller apartments (12

rooms instead of 25).
Includes Mr. & Mrs.
Norman Armour, Mr. &
Mrs. Norman Armour,
Jr., Mr. & Mrs. James
Bruce, Mrs. Percy
Ebbott, and Mrs.
Hamilton C. Clairborne.

820 Fifth Avenue
Like 834, one of the
most expensive places in
town. Residents include
Mr. William Paley, Mr.
& Mrs. William Burden,
Mrs. Armand Erpf and
Chauncey Stillman.

812 Fifth Avenue
The pride and joy of the
Nelson Rockefellers.

647 Fifth Avenue
The Olympic Tower,
dubbed "The Tower of
Power," was Aristotle
Onassis's pet project.
The most secure high-
rise in the world, tenants
pay $250,000-plus and
own their apartments.
Security consists of
bullet-proof windows,
bomb scanning devices,
and bodyguards. Even
tenants' paintings are
wired into the alarm
system, a system (run by
computer) that is

complex, to say the
least. And no wonder.
The list of tenants
includes princes,
princesses, sheikhs,
counts, duchesses, and
tycoons such as Gucci,
Rochas, Rothschild,
Khashoggi, Grant, and
Dillon.

1 West 72nd Street
In 1884 when The
Dakota was built,
snobby New Yorkers
said it was so far
uptown it might as well
be in Dakota—and
that's how it got its
name. It may be "west,"
but it's the "goldest"
west for luminaries such
as Gil and Susan Shiva,
Eugenia Sheppard,
Lauren Bacall, the
Warner Leroys, and Rex
Reed. The newest
apartment owner is King
Faisal and his retinue of
oasis refugees.

United Nations Plaza
They call this the high-
rise for over-achievers.
All the glass-plus
cooperatives overlook
the U.N., but there
aren't many diplomats

there. Residents include Gloria Vanderbilt Cooper, Walter Riston (First National City Bank), David Susskind, Gordon Parks, Truman Capote, and Mrs. Alice Fordyce.

1111 Park Avenue
An old-fashioned building. Home of Mr. & Mrs. Douglas Black and Mr. & Mrs. Louis Auchincloss.

888 Park Avenue
Not particularly glamorous, but nobody misses Kay Meehan's parties.

840 Park Avenue
Mr. & Mrs. Edward Chase rule the roost.

800 Park Avenue
When Stewart Mott moved in with his gardens, the place lost some of its stuffiness.

778 Park Avenue
Brooke Astor gives glamor to what was known as "the place where Bill Buckley lives."

740 Park Avenue
"It only takes money" to get in here—no social credentials needed. Saul Steinberg (Leasco Data Corp.) spent $1.5 million for 30 rooms and spent another million to decorate. Other millionaires included the Mahoneys, Bronfmans, Mrs. Ingersoll, and Mrs. Haupt.

720 Park Avenue
A very social place. Tucker, Havemeyer, Woolworth, Lynch, and Phipps are a few of the golden names.

580 Park Avenue
A huge place, stretching from 63rd to 64th, with lots of apartments filled with the likes of Roger Blough of U.S. Steel, John Olin of Olin Mathieson, and John Power of Pfizer.

The Waldorf Towers
Atop the Waldorf Astoria Hotel—some of the best views in town. Mrs. William Woodward now lives there, along with the MacArthurs,

Scalis, Hoovers, and
Rollinses.

1 Sutton Place
The hardest place in
town to get into—that
is, when there is a
vacancy. It's second only
to heaven. Some earthly
tenants are Mr. & Mrs.
Gilbert Chapman, Janett
Neff, Virgil Sherril, and
wonderful Mrs.
Woolcott Blair.

1 Beekman Place
A huge old fortress with
terraces instead of
canyons all over the
riverside. Big guns who
live there are John D.
Rockefeller III,
Huntington Hartford,
and the George
Boomers!

17 Beekman Place
This fine old brownstone
is still occupied by a

single "clout" family: the
Irving Berlins.

29 Beekman Place
The former Mary Lasker
town house is now the
residence of Princess
Ashraf Pahlavi of Iran
and her 13 body-
guards—whenever they
drop into New York.

River House
Not to be confused with
The River Club in the
same building. But the
memberships sometimes
are interchangeable.
Walter Hoving, E. F.
Hutton, Mrs. Harold
Vanderbilt, the Joshua
Logans, Mrs. Owen
Cheatham, for starters.

The Carlyle Hotel
Hideaway spot for all
big richies. Some co-ops.
Henry Ford and all that
wonderful group crowd
into the elevator.

One problem that faces the rich (no matter where they live)
is the constant fear of kidnappings.

"Assailants are more ruthless in the late seventies than they
have ever been before," explains James Bolduc, sales manager
for Protective Materials, one of the leading companies that
purvey maximum security. "So rich people need *our kind* of
safeguards to insure their peace of mind."

These strategies usually include surveillance by bodyguards (most often ex-FBI or Military Intelligence men and women) whose salaries range from $20,000 to $75,000 a year.

Posing as business associates of the head of the house, male guards will stay as close as possible to their client at all times while female counterparts, undercover as maids, shield the wife and children. Whole families usually carry ultra-sonic transmitters (that look exactly like felt-tip pens) to summon help from a Central Control Board if anything happens to these guards.

Some wealthier suburban households, the *New York Post* reported in February, 1978, are spending over $50,000 a year beyond the cost of bodyguards for more personal protection. They drive armor-plated cars (Mustangs or Volvos for the wives; Pontiacs or Buicks for the husbands) that cost about $38,000 per vehicle, not including shatterproof glass. Extras on these automobiles include: devices that scatter tacks in the path of a pursuing car; gunports; and smoke and tear gas canisters that can be triggered in the event of an ambush.

Detroit sources reveal there is even a remote-control monitoring device that when activated by a client (a quarter-mile away) checks to see that the motor has not been sabotaged with explosives. And, if all is well, the mechanism opens the car door and starts the ignition!

If all of the above sounds like Mafia-lifestyle gone manor-born, consider these wardrobe items favored by some worried capitalists: soft, bulletproof, unisex T-shirts, marketed from $80 to $180; and bulletproof purses and briefcases (to be held as a shield in case of a sudden attack) that start at $200.

It is fortifying a home that really runs up the security budget, however. Twenty-thousand dollars is a low estimate to "defense-system" a modest-sized dwelling, according to Fred Rayne, whose Florida-based Rayne International supplies at-home impregnability for most of the *poor, middle,* and *really-really rich* these chancy days.

"On top of that," says Rayne, "several of these houses (and a lot of New York cooperatives, too) have inner 'safe-rooms' that are invulnerable against hand-grenade attack or Molotov cocktails. In an emergency, a client enters one by simply working a combination code on his jacket buttons."

One owner of a large estate in Westchester was so concerned after the Bronfman kidnapping in 1976 that he installed a $275,000 computer system that checks out every movement at each window and door of his 36-bedroom mansion, besides recording and photographing any peregrinations in the driveway. All of that in addition to a 30-man security police force and 3 vicious guard dogs. But, oh well, every man ought to have the right to a little paranoia now and then.

V How You Can Tell Who Is Rich

*(Or . . . The Fellow at the Next Desk Might
Be a Rockefeller)*

All the really nice people are acting poor these days, as Mary
McCarthy observed in Britain at the close of World War II. But
with typical excess, the American rich take a mite too much
pleasure in their poverty. For one thing, everyone works these
days. And even royalty takes a turn punching the time clock!

Eugenia Sheppard recently chronicled that the most welcome endowment to New York's dwindling International Set was
the arrival to these shores of Countess Cristina and Count
Enrico di Carimate of Rome.

An extremely attractive young couple, who are both frankly
decorative as well as super-moneyed, Count Enrico's family
owns a string of factories that manufacture all manner of
hardware products while Countess Cristina's father is Italy's
helicopter king. The di Carimates emigrated to the U.S. from
their native land late in 1977 after a wave of terrifying socialite
kidnappings made them fearful for the welfare of their small
son, Ascanio.

As Eugenia pointed out, the presence of these regal refugees
in New York normally would transfuse new blood into the
"lunch bunch" who regularly meet at Orsini's for Carpaccio à la
Olio or, at the very least, set Southhampton hostesses to
rearranging their weekend guest lists. But that was not to be the
case.

The Count and Countess di Carimate accept social engage-
ments only before nine and after five . . . the business hours of
their thriving little jewelry boutique on Madison Avenue and
66th Street. For these jet-setters (like so many of the other new
traitors to their class) have become wage earners in earnest.

It is all part and parcel of a new wave of social
declassification—wherein the work ethic is decidedly more in
vogue than playing around. This behavior pattern, recent to the
rich, curiously seems rooted in the same anti-Establishment
convulsion that produced Flower Children, Weathermen, and the
Yippie movement a decade ago.

There are odder guidelines to be noted in the societal

upheaval among the upper classes, however. Besides working at full-time jobs or using their names as collateral for product syndication, as Gloria Vanderbilt has done so successfully, the rich now have begun to imitate the economies (and even the look) of the poor!

They have begun opting for small, servantless quarters; some even cook for themselves. And they decidedly dress down!

And there is not a jot of prestige loss for someone as upwardly mobile as C-Z Guest, for instance, to be seen having Maximillian restyle her last year's sable coat or Amanda Burden wearing the same ball gown (a Valentino, to be sure) twice in the very same season. The current crew of social swimmers all seem to sense that the *new* is not *necessary* for the maintenance of their images.

Actually, it has become quite smart among the younger upper set even to appear slightly impoverished. And *Women's Wear Daily* (though decrying a trend) proclaimed earlier this year that "Shabby Chic Is Still Definitely *In*."

Definitely *out* (and déclassé, besides) is any open display of ostentatious wealth. Truman Capote's fabulous (and very well-publicized) "Black and White Ball" at the Plaza Hotel—for several hundred of his intimate friends—might have been considered the height of style in the sixties but is merely chided as "income tax overkill" today!

In the late seventies it is considered deplorable to be that affluent. Or, to put it even more precisely, to be observed *acting* in such an overly affluent manner.

So it was not considered paradoxical to her peers that while Jacqueline Onassis received a purported $26 million settlement from stepdaughter Christina Onassis for renouncing further claim to her father's estate, she remained dutifully at her desk as Consulting Editor for Viking Press as the enormity of her demands rocked the rest of the nation.

Never once during the daily emblazonment of her legacy in the various media (rife with negative editorials about her role in the monetary transactions and damning her acquisitiveness) did Mrs. Onassis apparently consider leaving her post at Viking— she was too rich to do it properly.

According to her ex-assistant, Becky Singleton, "Jackie

worked in a small, almost Spartan office. She came to work most days in sweaters and slacks, wearing no jewelry, dressed exactly like the rest of us . . . except that somehow she managed to do it a little better." And even during the terrible hullabaloo in the press, Jackie always walked down the hall to the coffee machine and worked with her door wide open like everybody else!

"She did most of her own typing, too—placed her own telephone calls and handled her own files—which was terrific for me," reports Miss Singleton (now a full-fledged editor at Viking) "because I'm terrible at that sort of thing myself."

Mrs. Onassis's defiance of public opinion was obviously a personal demonstration of her independence, but it was also a manifest example of "shabby chic" in action. *Work conquers all* is the old proletarian battle cry.

When Mrs. O. finally relinquished her job, it was over an ethical conflict with Viking's management. The corporate decision to publish a novel about an assassination attempt on the life of a future American president (Edward Kennedy, by name) was a subject she considered untenable in light of her personal associations. She displayed a genteel demeanor of quite a different stripe than her intensive career involvement and her passionate struggle to maintain a "fair share" of her widow's right would seem to indicate.

After Mrs. Onassis's departure from Viking, newspapers throughout the country were filled with speculation about where the nation's No. 1 social butterfly-metamorphosed-into-business-executive would next alight.

Rumors proliferated that she would be offered Henry Geldzahler's post as Curator of the Metropolitan Museum of Art or be snared as Barbara Walters's replacement at ABC, but obviously the lady's heart was still in the publishing business. On February 14, 1978 (Valentine's Day), Jacqueline Onassis started a new job as Associate Editor for Doubleday and Company and now (according to her new assistant—who does type) has a pile of manuscripts at least four feet high on her desk!

According to the new sociologists, while the cult of the work ethic and the espousal of slightly dilapidated appurtenances might possibly become a true way of life for the very rich, this vogue appears to be, like all other behavior fads, merely a passing fancy—chiefly associated with dress and decoration.

In decorator terms, "shabby chic" means doing up your quarters in a very "lived-in" style. And while not mangy exactly, the look is definitely faded and worn, a mode of decor where nothing is particularly new and, definitely, nothing matches. Borrowing a leaf from the stoic British, the purveyors of this trend insist that the truly smartest furniture these days looks as if it had been inherited from some Great House where it was well cared for by a bevy of housemaids. But it also must look very well used and have the corners and nap rubbed off of everything.

Shabby chic dress has had a longer go-round with fashion leaders. The "peasant look" and the recycled "grab-bag" costume has had a decided popularity among young American trend-setters for years. In 1976 Yves St. Laurent put the ultimate stamp of his authority on this raggle-taggle style. But his long, rusty overblouses and romantic silken shawls draped over layers and layers of mock-tattered garments proved to be too uniquely haute couture to be acceptable as a fashion uniform among the new elite. They much preferred the modesty of their denim and patchwork or the "'30s thrift shop" assemblages so widely popularized by their own class designer, Diane von Furstenberg. For this look assures no social barricades whatsoever.

Interestingly enough, in his 1977 Paris collections, St. Laurent accepted the dictum. His new fashion line, he widely proclaimed, was inspired solely by New York's street look. In these uncertain times for the very rich, the upper classes not only want to look exactly like the lower but they also relish the cover of anonymity in the duplication.

It was not always so.

In the truly great old days of high society, a rigid caste system of birth and private education precluded any mixing up of who was who! Shopgirls and parlor maids might read of the luxe comings and goings of their betters in the Sunday rotogravure pages—but that was that.

Even if they secretly coveted some gown or cosmetic that the rich and famous established as *de rigeur* fashion in the shiny sheets of *Vogue, Harper's Bazaar,* or *Town & Country,* they had sparse hope of ever achieving their ends. For one thing, their station forbade the presumption and, for another, the marked differences in their incomes made emulation an impossibility.

As Mary McCarthy noted, "Forty years ago a copy of *Vogue* was on the sewing-room table of nearly every respectable middle-class American home. Provincial women with modest incomes pored over it to pick up 'hints,' and they carried it along to the family dressmaker, where they copied and approximated a dress yoke or a classic bit of fagoting almost with a sense of pilferage." The fashion ideas they lifted made the pulse of their Singers race in nervous daring and defiance. (What, oh what, would *Vogue* say if it knew?)

Today, quite in contrast, there is nothing much in the pages of *Vogue* that cannot be afforded by most of its largely middle-class readers.

Even those Paris couturier fashions (printed in super-urgent sneak preview sections twice a year), they surely know, will be available as "authenticated designer knock-offs" on the medium-priced racks of stores all over the country—practically by the time they have thumbed through the issue.

And the glossily photographed models (and, in *Town & Country's* case, moneyed maidens) who are the denizens of these still shiny sheets look not one whit more glamorous or essentially different from the matrons of middle America who peruse them between the hair dryer and the comb-out. In some instances models even appear less attractive (seemingly by design).

The cult of "looking the same as one's lessers" has afflicted the rich with a kind of aggressive paranoia. So it comes as no surprise to read, tucked away in Earl Wilson's syndicated gossip column, that:

> RICH GAL CHRISTINA ONASSIS is very
> proud of being pictured as a working
> girl who gets up in the morning and
> goes to her job. There's nothing
> frivolous about her. She works with
> the zeal of her late father, Ari. . . .

If the item caused few eyebrows to rise perceptibly, it is only because working-girl millionairesses are becoming common garden-variety phenomena in New York's business world. In May of 1977 *Women's Wear Daily* editorialized on the subject:

> Three years ago SA* turned a jet-setting Princess Diane von Furstenberg into a sultry cover-girl merchant of basic wrap dresses. Recently it turned Newport socialite Mary McFadden into a high priestess of evening exotica—and now Charlotte Ford into a cost-conscious entrepreneur of Ivy League sportswear.

Actually, so many of the country's wealthiest citizens seem to be filling out their F.S. 1 forms these days that the same chronicler of fashion and Fun-City doings, *WWD*, felt it incumbent to announce in a bannered feature: "These Are the BPs† Who Work." The following roster was arranged by vocational pecking order rather than social significance. But all were asked the same question: "Why do you work?"

GLORIA VANDERBILT COOPER
She's an "artist." In 1970, after two years with Hallmark Cards, she began designing home furnishings for Bloomcraft. In 1976 Gloria Vanderbilt, Ltd., was formed and her first collection shown. (Subsequently, Gloria Vanderbilt, Ltd., failed because of faulty business dealings and poor administrative operations, in 1977. But the invincible Gloria, though recently widowed, surfaced again and now, on Seventh Avenue in another guise, is Gloria Vanderbilt, Blouses.)
Why does she work?
"Because I'm a designer with tremendous drive to change the shape of the world. . . . I think of my name as only something I was born with. If my customers attach glamour to it, well, that's part of the response."

LEE RADZIWILL
President of Lee Radziwill, Inc., Interior Decorator. (Ex-actress, model, and Princess.)

---

*Seventh Avenue, certainly not sex appeal.
†Beautiful People

"Why do I work?"

"People say I have a knack for it. I can't understand everyone's surprise at my working. I have always been a participator, not an observer, and one needs to satisfy one's creative abilities."

DIANE VON FURSTENBERG

The most marketable female in fashion since Coco Chanel, according to *Newsweek* magazine. Her high-cheeked, wide-mouthed portrait peers out from every tag on every Diane von Furstenberg dress—and her distinctive signature is implanted on her cosmetics, perfumes, furs, jewelry, handbags, shirts, scarves, shoes, and sunglasses. (Her personal corporation, of which she is the principal stockholder, owns her dress firm as well as the cosmetic and perfume operations. The rest are produced under lucrative licensing arrangements—and the royalties are rumored to be mind-boggling at the moment.)

Miss von Furstenberg also juggles broadcasting into her busy schedule. She can be heard over CBS Newsradio three times a week, talking up chic chit-chat.

Why does she work?

"I didn't want to have to ask anything from anyone else. There are so many useful things to do if you don't need the money. Work gives me identity!"

CHARLOTTE FORD

President and integral design force at her own firm, Charlotte Ford, Inc., where she works five days a week.

"People who make negative remarks about me are just jealous. I invested half of the money in this company. Why would I do a halfhearted job? That would be like throwing money down the drain. And no one in America has that privilege . . . particularly not a Ford!"

Miss Ford is a more dedicated business person than most of her jet-set pals suspect. Between the production of her current "fall line," she also managed to write a book for Simon and Schuster called *Modern Manners* and to split from her second husband, Tony Forstmann. An interesting side-note to her personal problems, the industrious lady has also written a series of articles for *Ladies Home Journal* on the subject, entitled: "How to Sensibly Handle a Divorce"!

MARY McFADDEN

Social Registerite, ex-*Vogue* editor, Miss McFadden was only eighteen when she first became a designer (for Dior in Paris). Now ensconced in an exotic loft on Seventh Avenue, her most recent collection, according to Eugenia Sheppard, " . . . proves that she's one of the most imaginative designers in the industry."

Why does she work?

"I don't know actually . . . there's so much money involved, it frankly makes me a little nervous to think about it!"

MICA ERTEGUN

Along with Chessy Raynor, she heads up MAC II, New York's most prestigious interior design and decorating firm, whose satisfied clientele includes Saks Fifth Avenue, the Carlyle Hotel, the Olympic Towers, and apartments of such notables as Jerome Robbins and the Shah of Iran.

"I started in this business because friends asked me to do their apartments and we (Chessy and I) were looking for something to do.

"We didn't take it very seriously and we made a lot of mistakes in the beginning. My husband was very amused, but he approved of the venture."

Though Mrs. Ertegun hardly needs the money she earns, she responds to the challenge implicit in the question: Why do you work?

"To make money. I'd hate to work and not make anything . . . because it seems so sort of dilettantish."

AHMET ERTEGUN

Mica's husband has a different work philosophy. "I never think of myself as a millionaire," he says. "What's a millionaire anyway? I can claim that I've made a million dollars a year for nearly fifteen years—but so what? My family always had money!"

Ertegun's late father was a Turkish Ambassador to the U.S. A charming capitalist, as well as an obvious *bon vivant,* son Ahmet spun his way to the top by capitalizing on his lifelong hobby of jazz—and his predilection for the "new sounds of the sixties." His company, Atlantic Records, has been in the forefront of developing new singing talent and rock groups for over a decade. And seems bigger than ever at the present moment.

Why does he work?

"Why do I? Why does anyone? It keeps you alive!"

PETER PULITZER

Palm Beach's playboy tycoon. He is the grandson of newspaper
millionaire and prize-bestower, Joseph Pulitzer, and former
husband of Lilly Pulitzer (an *avant garde* member of the "pretend
proletariat," whose famous shop became a rich supermarket on
Worth Avenue in Palm Beach and Job's Lane in Southampton in
the sixties, and whose name is forever immortalized in the little
nothings the rich wear at play, called "Lillys"). Peter and Lilly
were married for 17 years before their divorce in 1969, but ever
since the split, Peter has become as well known for his multiple
business talents as his former wife for her chic.

A most intrepid entrepreneur, Pulitzer is heavily into the
resort trade (Doherty's Grill Room, an eating house-pub smack in
the center of Palm Beach, a big motor lodge in Miami Beach, a
new restaurant in Fort Meyers called O'Bannons, plus a packing-
house and a huge citrus grove in the middle of the state). Pulitzer
also owns a string of hotels in Amsterdam and used to jet
regularly to another he had picked up in Djakarta—until the
wear and tear of it all finally tempered his taste for overseas
commerce.

Why does he work?

"To pay for my habit . . . which is playing around." But a
friend of his amended that answer somewhat. "Peter is a real
playboy, all right. But he plays at making money!"

C-Z GUEST

Mrs. Winston F. C. Guest, one of the truly great beauties of our
time and a seemingly permanent fixture on all the really important lists (the *Social Register* and the "Best Dressed," etc.), was
born Lucy Cochrane in Boston and led a typically proper Back
Bay-Brahmin girl existence until she married patrician Winston
Guest, at which time, as *Time* magazine reported, she inherited
the mantle of Social Leader Numero Uno in America's waning
aristocracy, a title she added to her myriad other occupations:
wife, mother, hostess, gardener, horse-breeder, and dog lover.

A darling of the glossy magazines since the late fifties
(probably because she is so damn photogenic), Mrs. Guest's
persona has now become so visible it is no longer necessary for
editors to identify her in text or captions by anything other than
her hyphenated initials.

With such weighty media prominence, it was inevitable that
she would be drawn into the merchandising of her name. The

publication of a book, *First Gardens,* was the initial step. Two years later, C-Z has become such a successful business-venturer that she does not rule out the idea of eventually becoming a vast conglomerate.

After her book's publication, she found herself in great demand as a lecturer at Garden Clubs all over the country. Then, in 1976, with a major chemical firm, she developed a heavily scented insect repellent, appropriately named "C-Z," that, according to advertising blurbs, "bugs hate but humans adore!" It took off as well.

"I found that once you get started, things happen to you," Mrs. Guest says.

Her latest project is an environmental complex: furniture created to her specification and constructed in Italy, an Interior Design and Decorating Service for industry and individual needs as well, and a line of unique children's fashions called, most naturally, "C-Z Baby."

Why does she work?

"Because it has opened a whole new world for me. Now, professionals receive me as if I were one of them . . . and believe me, I am!"

LORNA LIVINGSTON
A direct descendant of the most prominent family in New York (six Livingstons were among the original so-called "Four Hundred"), Miss Livingston is one of the anonymous rich employees that abound in New York's current business scene. Until recently, she was the Managing Editor of "Manhattan East," an upper-East-Side weekly newspaper, where she shuffled features about the police system, local politics, decorators, and diplomats with equal ease.

A tall, tawny blonde, whose Beekman Place "coming-out" party and debut was well splashed over the society pages of every newspaper in the country 20 years ago, she has no time in her life now for such events, or any old-time club ties that her family helped institute and perpetuate.

"That kind of thing is really passé. Besides, it costs a lot," says Miss Livingston, closing the subject. She has been a working woman for years.

Why does she work?

"Why? The same reason I brush my teeth. It's a good habit— and it prevents decay."

WARNER LEROY

Scion to the legendary Warner Brothers fortune (grandson of founder Harry Warner and son of famed movie director Mervyn Leroy), Warner Leroy is a familiar figure (if a rather largish one) at every Fancy Dress event and press-covered reception that takes place in New York. A one-time theatrical impresario and failed director, his track record improved immeasurably when he left show biz for the equally flashy world of eats.

Something of a *gourmand,* he is a restaurateur of note, and two of his establishments are virtually landmarks among N.Y.'s cognoscenti. Maxwell's Plum is the mint version of a swinging singles bar—but the quality of the food and the majesty of the decor is so overwhelming it eases the pain of the establishment's purpose. It also happens to be a wild money-maker for sole owner Leroy. Tavern-on-the-Green is the old Central Park landmark, but so chivvied and jazzed-up Boss Tweed would never recognize the joint. It is all splendor and gourmetry and the reservation list is one week long, Mr. Leroy's aides report.

Recently, this magna-mogul added a new string to his diversionary bow. He has announced that he plans a Maoist Pleasure Palace (Chinese food) right next door to the Plum.

Certainly not an average businessman executive, Warner Leroy is intellectual, cherubic in appearance, with large horned-rim glasses that give him a perpetually perplexed Joe College air. He favors a wildly impressionistic wardrobe, usually cut velvet or upholstery fabric suits (by Meledandri) rather than any of the basic blues favored by his executive comperes. But make no mistake about Warner Leroy, his heart belongs to the Daedaleans.

Why does he work?

"F.U.N. Listen, it helps to have the money to begin with, but the fun is doing what I'm doing. What more can I say?"

One employment option long open to the rich has been the editorial departments of major fashion magazines. For years and years, the mentors of glossy publications like *Vogue, Town & Country,* and *Harper's Bazaar* felt that the inclusion of socially accepted names on a masthead established a sense of sorority between the magazine and its prime subscribers. The late Barbara Cushing Paley, for instance, usually credited her unique fashion sense (nominated as one of the best-dressed women of the world fourteen times) to knowledge acquired during a nine-year stint at *Vogue.*

"But," according to one ex-*Harper's Bazaar* staffer (now a senior editor at a non-fashion publication), "the Paleys are far and few between.

"When I worked at *Bazaar,* most of these snobby girls came and went like very small blasts of hot air! Hired to snare other socialites for photography, they usually considered that assignment demeaning and tried to get us non-U types to do all their dirty work. Eventually they drifted off. . . . Palm Beach or the Caribbean in February when New York was too snowy—you know the syndrome! Or else top management, realizing the error of such employment, assigned them to Siberia—the traveling fashion shows sent to department stores *all* over the country. That cross-country trek most often ended all their careers in publishing!"

One notable exception (according to *Bazaar* lore) was the rigid tenure of Nan (Mrs. Thomas) Kempner as Associate Fashion Editor at the magazine.

"Nan was certainly not bad at her job, but after a discreet time her usefulness was equated with the size of her salary, and the powers-that-be decided to ease her out!

"First she was given the cross-country treatment, but she performed all those chores nobly—without a sign of defection. Next she was assigned to cover the underwear market—always a downer, but no duty at the magazine seemed too degrading or trivial for her full attention. Only when *Bazaar* moved from their tiny old offices on Madison and Fifty-sixth Street to the grand spaces they now occupy at 717 Fifth Avenue did Nan have her real trial by fire. For it became instantly apparent to everyone who the true brass was, by the size and location of the offices. People with clout had windows facing the street; super clouts had two windows and a view of Fifth Avenue besides. Nan's office was one of the smallest: deep in the bowels, next to the Xerox room.

"Everyone at *Bazaar* knew this was a killing blow. But Nan never flinched at the size or position of her quarters. She just kept working, rushing about (in her hat of course) as if she faced all of Central Park.

One night after work, however, she had her tiny office

entirely redecorated—by Billy Baldwin, no less. No one knew how it was managed, but by next morning the little hen coop had been mirrored and covered with ultra-suede from floor to ceiling; a drab desk replaced by a slab of snowy marble; indirect lighting—the works. A triumph of design. Entirely paid for by Nan Kempner!

The day after, she sent the management a letter of resignation."

Other novitiates to the list of "Worker-rich" have less sensibility perhaps, but the desire for recognition (on a job well done) is still coeval.

To unseat the other corporate princesses perhaps, yet another royal Diane (Princess de Beauvau), who is the 22-year-old granddaughter of Antenor Patino, one of the richest men in the whole wide world, recently made her debut as a fashion designer on Seventh Avenue.

After a posh opening at the Plaza's Terrace Room, Eugenia Sheppard noted that Halston refused even to show his face at the Collection—while C-Z beamed beatifically through it all. And Grandpa Patino jetted in from Paris on his private 707 just so he could drop off some gold and diamond baubles (from Van Cleef) as goodluck charms, which certainly did not hurt the press coverage either. Cash registers have been ringing happily ever after.

Industry is the alternate lifestyle to indolence everywhere one looks. Bobo Rockefeller, we hear on very good authority, is seriously writing a cookbook, and Lord Colin Campbell (whose older brother recently became the Duke of Argyll and inherited Inverary Castle) has just found a perfect little pad in New York (away from the hurly-burly of the Castle and his other island hideaway on Fiji) just so he can finish the gothic novel he is writing. Lucky Lynn Revson (widow of Revlon's ducal founder, Charles Revson) has had *her* book published already. A prestigious tome ($16.95), with a cover photograph by Richard Avedon, no less, it is entitled *Lynn Revson's World of Style*. And since Lynn taped it into a cassette rather than writing it down, the result is a very free-form "you and I" style, according to advance reports.

Mrs. Revson tells her readers all sorts of useful information, such as how to wear a smashing ruby or emerald with their T-shirts and jeans and how to decorate their apartments with white orchids for a really important dinner party—which is bound to make the book a bible for every working girl! Particularly ones like Diane, Gloria, Lee, Charlotte, and Mica . . . and that's all she wrote!

VI Who's Upstairs and Who's Downstairs?

(Or . . . What Happened to the Ruling Class?)

The caterer always has a tale to tell.

Some years back when I plied my cooking talents in the lusher outposts of Long Island and Manhattan, I once was summoned to a pre-party interview with a well-publicized hostess (who shall be nameless here for propriety's sake).

She was rich and recently divorced and, though obviously traumatized by a hangover during our endless discussion of the pros and cons of hot hors d'oeuvre versus cold, appeared to be an eminently desirable client for me to name-drop afterward.

There were certain drawbacks to being in her employ even temporarily, however, that could not be ignored. She drank, lived in Connecticut, and bred prize Siamese cats—crotchets not insurmountable in themselves, but coupled with her aggressive manner and a tendency to bargain, they proved a deadly combination.

"You people are *so* expensive," she whistled as she examined the standard pre-prandial estimate. "I don't know if I can really afford your services."

This, after two meetings on her Greenwich turf just to examine the kitchen and its kitty-littered facilities.

"But you are so highly recommended I guess I might as well chance it this time. You will come in and do the main course and dessert," she announced, "and I will do the rest."

A blue pencil was produced.

"Canapés are simply never eaten so they are just a waste of your time and *my money!*" she said, crossing them off the proffered menu.

"My girl will get some nuts and olive 'thingees' at the Superette, instead. I always do the fish course myself, anyway, because I am actually rather famous for my salmon mousse. And that will make things easier all around."

She studied the list again.

"No soup. No bread and butter. And no cheese and fruit." She smiled as she patted a particularly mettlesome young

Siamese cat who was climbing up my pant leg. "Too much food deadens a good party in the final analysis!"

Salad?

"Of course. But what *is* salad anyway? You bring the dressing and I'll do the greens. Agreed?"

Agreed. With pain in the pocketbook but unquestioning acquiescence on my part, I took my leave.

On the day of the event the hostess was bedded down with what her maid proclaimed "a light-type virus" while I commandeered her kitchen for action.

Hired help appeared and the tables were set—even the Chateaubriands were braised before the lady finally made her entrance, blanched but red-eyed in the inevitable Pucci of that season. A trail of adoring if enigmatic cats followed in her wake.

Everything is in order, I nodded, as she poked into the various steaming skillets and porringers.

"It looks quite nice. Umh. . . . "

"Except for your mousse."

"My what?"

"The fish course. The one you are famous for!"

"My God," she groaned. "I knew I forgot something. Get me a martini—and a flashlight." This last, barked to her obliging black maid. "No, no. The flashlight first, dummy!"

As I watched, the cats parted before her as if by intuition. She advanced to her freezer and with much hacking and swearing produced from its depths a retrograde copper mold, completely swathed in layers of plastic wrap and thin ice.

"I made this last August when the bass were running. Or perhaps it was the year before. We all got so sloshed at dinner it never was served. You think it's any good?"

Together we both sniffed at the icy gray salvage.

It didn't smell rancid.

"Well, that's always the test, isn't it? Let's just unmold it—and later your people can run a little chopped parsley over the top. Perhaps, umh . . . a ring of cherry tomatoes for some color. . . . "

Madame placed the empty but still congealed copper form on the floor where a small Siamese was half asleep, curled up beside the gleaming Garland range.

"Have a taste, darling," she cooed, as the kitten surveyed the cold metal with her tongue. "Yes, num num."

"It's perfectly fine, you see," she announced to me. "She likes it! Everyone knows cats never eat *anything* that isn't perfectly good for them!"

The guests at her dinner party, accustomed to her Spartan fare, relished the first course. Plates were scraped practically clean before they returned to the pantry.

The hostess was in fine fettle. The drinks had been long and numerous and the wine chilled to exactly the perfect degree to complement her mousse, she declared as she sailed into the kitchen to order up another bottle.

"Everything is divine. Divine," she murmured throatily as she made a mid-meal inspection between courses. Spearing a carrot strip, she even smiled waggishly at her caterer.

"You must teach me your trick with vegetables. I adore them this way! So crisp. So divine. . . . "

Patting the pride of sleek amber animals that always seemed to surround her, she prodded them away from me (the flambéeing *saucier*) to the safety of the back porch, where an enormous sandbox was permanently filled with Kleen Kitty.

"Oh, my God!" she shrieked at the kitchen door.

My flame went out abruptly as the rest of the staff of hired hands, galvanized by her cry, drew close to offer some assistance.

"It killed her!" she screamed at us all. "The mousse killed her!"

There, on the darkened porch floor, lay a very small and inert Siamese kitten, unmistakably stretched in *rigor mortis*. Dead as a proverbial doornail.

"Oh, my God," she repeated to herself as the realization finally hit home. "It will kill them all!"

Racing to the kitchen phone, with some assistance, she

dialed her personal physician. Wringing her bejeweled wrists before the connection could be made, she groaned, "Listen to them all in there . . . laughing!"

On hearing her terrible tale, the doctor unequivocally determined that she must rush all her guests to the Greenwich Hospital—a 20-minute drive from her estate—to have their collective stomachs pumped.

"Darling," she whispered to me, "I am going to die. Die right here and now." Handing me the phone, she commanded, "Dial 911. And order an ambulance immediately. And make it a *large* one!"

I did. As she, fortified by straight gin now, went back into her dining room to make the dire facts known to Connecticut's finest families.

The party can be said to have ended for this caterer on a *high* note: the ultra-sonic wail of a police siren and two ambulances speeding away down the darkened Post Road.

All the glamorous party fold, shepherded in tandem onto mobile cots and army blankets, sat grim-eyed and glassy in their assorted tartan dinner jackets and Valentino caftans. The tainted food obviously had come from the purveyor of the provender, in their minds. So no name-dropping success would ever be accrued from this assignment.

By the late hour, a sober hostess returned (in a taxi and quite alone). The filet of beef was long past being *à point* and was now wrapped in aluminum foil for safekeeping. The kitchen was spotless, however, all the uneaten food stacked in plastic containers in the refrigerator. Only the dessert, a sumptuous *tarte à l'orange,* waited to be housed. Surely Madame didn't wish it in the same lethal freezer?

The lady couldn't have cared less.

"I don't care where you shove it. Frankly I detest sweets, anyhow. Take it with you—for all of me, darling!" she said. *"Quelle dommage*—no matter how one looks at it! *N'est-ce pas?"* She crooned to her remaining brood of cats as she poured herself fresh gin.

"Just clear the decks, and send me a bill!"

The bill was duly sent but never paid—or, to put it more

precisely, not quite ever paid in full! The charge for the hired help was satisfied, but the amount due for their service was arbitrarily slashed in half since the party ended on such an abrupt note. The food costs, however, were permanently withheld—as a recrimination for being party to a forever maligned social occasion.

Almost a year later, after two large and reputable collection agencies refused a bid to represent me in this matter, a very well-known and prestigious New York lawyer called, ostensibly to discuss the repercussions a small-claims trial might have on my reputation as a rising caterer.

"Off the record, I would advise you to settle the matter," he suggested, naming a figure considerably less than the original outlay for groceries.

"Gossip can be ruinous among these queens of love and beauty, after all."

I agreed with him, knowing full well that any smoking pistol that turned up would doubtless become my own. The conversation that followed was all affability; he was a charming man, and he and his wife (Westchesterites) also gave parties from time-to-time, so he quite empathized with the caterer's plight.

"The damndest thing about that disastrous dinner party is probably something you don't know," he allowed after a bit. "The cat didn't die of tainted mousse at all. No . . . no!" He interrupted himself to chuckle over the phone. "It was run over in the driveway by one of the guests' chauffeurs. A sensitive fellow, he hadn't wanted to spoil the party, so he left the poor bugger on the back porch instead. We didn't actually find out the truth for, oh, at least a week or so later. But that's how these things go, y'know. . . . "

Indeed I do!

* * *

The point of this tale, obscured by my wayward biography perhaps, is that there is no longer any "downstairs world" of protective servants left to insulate the rich life.

More and more grand households are being run with

minimal staffs, and ever-established pillars of society (well known to us from Suzy-and-Eugenia lore) are forced to make do on their own—with some assists from proliferating gourmet take-out foods and a weekly cleaning service. Because servants, even if they can be afforded, are simply no longer available.

As a matter of fact, the trend toward "come-in" staffs has grown so that in Washington Mrs. Robert Kinther said: "You see a friend's face only occasionally at dinner, but you see the same caterers and maids night after night!" "On the East Side," confirms New York man-about-town Drew Dudley, "the same butlers greet you at household after household."

The average cook (chef) for a small Park Avenue family back in 1948 earned something less than $100 a week, plus food and lodging, of course. Even considering the dramatic inflationary rise in our standard of living since then, the wage escalation in that profession is absolutely astonishing. The same kitchen worker could not be hired on the open market today for less than $400 a week, plus the increment of shopping privileges—which automatically swells that income by 15 percent at the very least. (This figure represents the untaxable percentage that is considered a standard perk all domestic service people receive from their major suppliers.)

But even at that healthy rate of recompense, turnover in the chefs' market is fast and furious. The good practitioners most often are snared by high-priced restaurants willing to double or even triple their wage scale because the pickings are so slim. Or they are pirated by upper-class raiders who offer private houses for living quarters and, in some cases, private schools for their children's educations.

I myself once was offered a $500 weekly stipend to join Mick Jagger's establishment as his personal chef (both here and wherever his footloose fancy happened to take him next). And rock stars aren't even designated, properly, *poor rich!*

I declined the bid out of misguided ethics and the belief that it was better to slave (and sometimes starve) on your own turf than be up for grandiose grabs! A philosophy, I am afraid, that infects all such entrepreneurism fated for non-survival.

Servant problems traditionally have dogged the rich, but the escalating rate of remuneration for service (inflated by new millionaires such as Mr. J.) has positively accelerated the old classic struggle. And it is not surprising to discover a whole new standard of employee-employer relations in those great households with the wherewithal to be able to command multi-person staffs—with labor dictating most of the terms.

In this equitable society, city servants are quite capable of refusing summer sojourns at their master's country establishment because *they* do not care for constrictive ex-urban isolation.

As a matter of fact, most reputable employment agents these days submit forms (to be filled out and co-signed by prospective employers), indicating that any "undue physical relocation on the part of a wage earner will be compensated for by supplementary interim income . . . to equalize the hardship of a residence change." And no maid worth her hire would consider taking a job in Greenwich, Connecticut, without first being assured of a paid-up charge account at the local taxi company.

It has been part of my own experience to note that hired live-in cooks no longer prepare food for large dinner parties. Declaring that extracurricular functions require the services of professionals (used to the trauma of multiple oven operations), the average chef puts a foot down on any number over six for dinner. And gets away with it!

Nor will the kitchen staff even consider assisting at those parties where outside help *is* employed.

"It's not the function of my job," a Swedish-born chef established at a splendid East-Side kitchen reported to me on one occasion.

"If a cook like me permits himself to be sucked into helping out at parties and these big dinners . . . *they* begin to expect it all the time! Before you know it, my status goes down—they ask me to go to the store or drive the car. Bake cakes, even! No thanks, I'd rather watch TV!"

Fifty years ago, the late Charles Ingersoll (of the imposing Philadelphia Ingersolls) managed to run his Penllyn House with only nine in help: a cook, chauffeur, butler, two maids, and a young footman for household chores plus two gardeners and a handyman for outside work.

Tall tales still are recounted of the domestic pride that these working members of the Ingersoll staff shared with their employer. Unbidden, the gardeners would re-rake all the winding gravel driveways each time a vehicle departed from the house, and every foot of grass would be cut by hand—then measured to make sure the turf was completely symmetrical on either side of the path.

Stephen Birmingham, who visited the same Penllyn establishment in the late 1960s, reported that Mr. Ingersoll's son John and his wife, far from inspiring like acts of selfless devotion from *their* personnel, were busily replacing a hundred or so feet of worn iron fencing about the property themselves.

"Because good help is so impossible to come by these days!"

If 1928 may be considered the optimum buyer's market for household help (with 57 domestic employment agencies recorded in the *Manhattan Telephone Directory* for that year as compared to a mere 7 in the latest listings), 1978 may be designated the nadir.

Miss Eileen [sic] at A. E. Johnson Employment (a blue-ribbon domestic purveyor in Manhattan) airily announced that a six-month wait for a cook or butler combination was not an unreasonable hiatus for a prospective employer *these days*.

"These days" was the key phrase in all of our conversational interchange.

"*These days* the best couples are still imported, but most often the only ones we are able to acquire are from Spain or North Africa. Unfortunately, no Danish, Swedish, or Norwegian personnel at all *these days!*"

Later, she explained that the skyrocketing inflation of the Scandinavian countries (once the prime tap for foreign-born household help) has made emigration to the U.S. unthinkable since even unskilled workers there are being paid twice what the best paid domestic receives here "these days."

Posing as a friend of a new town-house owner, I made

several discreet inquiries about what is needed to run a basic New York establishment.

"A cook-houseman (live-in) and a maid (come-in) plus a daily worker to do the heavy cleaning," was the barest set of domestic essentials she could envision.

When asked what the average salaries for a staff of three such household workers would be, the lady began to laugh nervously.

"Oh my, that is a loaded question. It depends on what one considers average. Anything . . . anything is possible *these days,* you know." Rifling through her files for a moment, she finally chose a pink card at random.

"We have just received a top-notch applicant. A young man with the very highest credentials imaginable. Palm Beach, Beverly Hills . . . the best names for references, but I think he is out of your friends's range."

What is his asking price?

"Well, that is always negotiable but upward of twenty-five, I would say, to start. Thirty thousand and one could be sure he would really settle in!"

And a maid? What is the going rate for them?

"Caucasion or black?"

Is there a price difference?

"Certainly not. But as there are no American girls listed with us at the moment, I thought I might make some discreet inquiries—if you would consider someone from the islands, say . . . ."

English speaking?

"Not always . . . *these days.*"

The salary, please.

"Eight hundred a month is the minimum listing for that service here. Employer pays the fee, of course."

Of course. *These days. . . .*

The daily worker was the only servant listed at what might be considered a bargain rate of $4.50 per hour with a minimum base employment of half-day (5 hours) plus carfare and lunch money.

Something money obviously cannot buy is *loyalty* from the servant class. The ratio of turnover among domestic employees is far greater than in any other job market in the United States today.

Why this mass abdication of the household in a time of increasing financial benefits and labor-saving appliances designed to make the life less burdensome? Why, indeed, the proliferating shortage of good domestics?

Reasons boil down to the lack of status inherent in all such employment. The stigma of servitude still clings to household occupations like the terrible smell of last night's lamb chops— even though most practitioners in the field are better paid than their fellow white collar workers.

Lures (such as lavish presents, cruises, color TVs, foreign vacations, stock market tips, tax help, and *these days* even medical insurance and pension plans) are regularly proffered by the rich to deodorize their servants' psyches. But without notable success. The rise of universal education, coupled with Women's Liberation and the Equal Rights Amendment, has besmirched forever the conceit of a healthy (if inflated) upstairs/downstairs society.

How do the rich *cope* in this era of vanished family retainers when every new day begins with only instant coffee and the promise of continued under-indulgence at the hands of their servitors? With diverse *modi operandi*, as they always have used in the face of communal adversity.

Mrs. Arthur Stanton, discovering that her newly arrived Spanish couple neither spoke English nor were capable of producing anything more elaborate than *arroz con pollo* or *gazpacho* for her East Hampton soirees, managed a crash course at Berlitz for herself (and the best gourmet cooking school in New York for signora). In six months they were all surviving admirably—until one of Mrs. Stanton's acquaintances discovered the cook and butler's manifest virtues one fateful afternoon at lunch. Pronouncing them "perfect gems," the lady conspired to snare them away from their protectress between the salad course and the mousse!

Mrs. Stuart Ingersoll's personal maid (who is a treasure, it is bruited about) fancied the decor of her mistress's newly funished bedroom so much it made her dissatisfied with her own quarters in the house. Before the little darling had a complete emotional crisis, Mrs. Ingersoll consulted her own psychiatrist about the matter. Relating "performance of duty as a loving servant" to similar performance as a loving friend, he came up with the diagnosis of "situational schizophrenia," which, if left unchecked, could lead to deep depression and separation. The treatment was relatively simple: a call to Billy Baldwin. Now Mrs. I.'s personal maid has an adjoining bedroom that's the twin of her own. *And everybody's happy!*

The Armand Erpfs were a December-May romance with a decided servant problem. Married when Mr. Erpf was in his seventies and Mrs. Erpf had just turned thirty, they both maintained admirable household establishments—leftover from their previous lives. They tried combining staffs but it wouldn't work. Each, you see, was possessed of an old family retainer: a housekeeper who absolutely detested her counterpart on sight. The Erpfs (peaceable types) solved the problem by living apart. They seem reasonably happy and have even produced an heir recently, thanks to Thursday nights and Sunday afternoons (the servants' days off.)

Mrs. T. Edward Chase is a well-known party-giver, but she knows exactly to what limits she can (and cannot) push her household staff. Mrs. Chase always has a caterer in attendance to perform all culinary exercises, and by and large she is satisfied with the results. But caterers never seem to leave the kitchen as precisely immaculate as Mrs. Chase's cook-housekeeper likes it. So, inevitably at a party's close, Mrs. Chase peels off the yard or so of Cartier diamonds she wears and, exchanging Givenchy and St. Laurent for Comet and Mr. Clean, she spruces up the galley to meet her domestic staff's requirements. Now that is truly coping!

The ultimate "coper" of them all is undoubtedly Jackie Onassis. Seared by cooks, butlers, and a raft of backstairs maids (who signed contracts for exposé books before their uniforms were properly unpacked), Mrs. O. has had a loyalty oath prepared by her lawyers, which all prospective house personnel must sign prior to their engagement. No books, talk shows, interviews, or movie deals . . . in perpetuity!

According to the last census report, there are only some 169,680 private-household workers who live in their employers' homes at the present time. If one adds up the total aggregate rich (as limned in this book)—150,000 *poor rich,* 75,000 *middle-class rich,* and 25,000 *really-really rich*—the figures apportion out to only one and one-half live-in servants per millionaire. Or that's what the census seems to imply.

Obviously, at current wage scales some of the *really-really rich* must be doing without. What follows are average wage rates compiled early in 1978 from some of the favored employment agencies* in New York City, where prices might be the country's highest.

WAGES THAT RICH ARE PAYING FOR SERVICE "THESE DAYS"

Governess, live-in	$150-$170/week
Babysitter, come-in	$3/hour
Butler, live-in	$7,500-$12,000/year and up
Butler, come-in	$5.50-$8/hour
Caterer	$15-$50 per head, per meal
Chauffeur, live-in or live-out	$175-$200/week
Chef, live-in	$10,000-$40,000/year
Cleaning, heavy work, come-in	$4.50/hour
Companion, live-in	$7,500-$10,000/year
Couple, live-in	$12,000-$20,000/year
Baby nurse	$150-$175/week
Guard, live-in	$200/week and up
Guard, come-in	$7/hour (plus expenses) and up
Jet pilot	$40,000-$65,000/year
Yacht captain	from $10,000/year

---

*Compiled from Anne Andrews Employment Agency; Chauffeurs Unlimited, Inc.; Finnish Employment Agency; A. E. Johnson Employment Agency, Inc.; Maids Unlimited, Inc; Sampson Employment Agency; Taylor Maid Service, Inc.

Laundress, live-in	from $125/week
Laundress, come-in	$35/day
Valet, live-in	$500-$1,000/month to start
Maids, live-in:	
Personal maid	$600/month
All-purpose maid	$500/month
Chambermaid	$500-$600/month
Kitchenmaid	$400-$500/month
Bar man, come-in	$15/hour
Waiters, come-in	$40/4-hour period, time-and-a-half after
Social secretary	$250-$300/week

The new breed of servant (making an executive salary) has caused an industrial revolution in the homemaking of the rich. Microwave ovens flower in every kitchen where once the Garlands grew. And pre-packaged entertainment is the rule of thumb for any social occasion.

Today, everything from breakfast in bed to a 200-person buffet for the Shah of Iran is catered (and cleaned up afterward) by staffs of bright and beautiful domestics who probably went to Harvard and Bennington with the host's children.

The following is a choice plateful of consigned party experts who fete America from quiche to shining quiche!

NEW YORK

Donald Bruce White Caterers, Inc.
From 4 to 400. One of the most experienced around.

Maurice Moore-Betty
$40 per person, average, but divorced persons are, for some reason, strictly taboo. Not your average fare.

Glorious Food
Chris Idone and Sean Driscoll whip up all manner of French-oriented food for all kinds of events. Booked months in advance, they check you and your kitchen out before they agree to do anything.

NEW YORK *Continued*

Peking Park Avenue Restaurant

Mr. Ting delivers Chinese banquets, but only in Midtown. Too much travel ruins the food, says he.

Stephen K. Bierman

A self-proclaimed "hors d'ouevres specialist," his goodies are famous all over town. Every party is "custom-designed."

Carolyn and Lawrence Noveck

The darlings of the Seventh Avenue set. (Carolyn was a former Coty Award winner, Carolyn Schnurer.) Their desserts are the *crème de la crème.*

Whitney Warren

Pheasant under glass for 3,000? Whitney (of the Main Line banking family) has done several and is *the* person to call for such arduous undertakings.

Bill Proops

A director of Lehman Brothers, Bill moonlights on weekends. A graduate of Ecole

Hôteliers of Lausanne, Switzerland, his "elegant" dinners cost $60 per. Jean-Jacques Bloos (who was the late Babe Paley's favorite florist) will apply his magic for an additional fee.

Mr. Babbington & Friend, Inc.

Joseph Ancel (there is no Mr. Babbington) will do the works for about $50 per person. His biggest was for 1,000 people: a Rolling Stones bash for Jimmy Carter.

Maison Germaine

The favorite of the "young" Clout Crowd, Germaine did Queen Frederick's reception and Mark Goodson's bash for Princess Margaret and ex-hubby Lord Snowdon.

Rudolph Stanish

Rudi works mainly in New York but *will* travel (with his pans and burners). You're not anyone unless Rudi has been in your kitchen omeleting his way (and yours) into oblivion.

Eleanor Rogers

Eleanor and partner Michael Guiton's quiches are famous in New York circles. Brunches start at $30 and go up, up, up.

Ralph Lupoli

For the casual affair, an *elegant* pizza party.

BOSTON

Silent Chef Caterers, Inc.

James Linnehan and crew make their own bread, *perfect* pâté, and marvelous meals. And for the Beacon Hill crowd, he has the finest crystal, china, and linens on hand for special occasions.

Legal Sea Foods

Bostonians hold this monstrous restaurant to be the ultimate in seafood. George Berkowitz delivers, and the price "ain't bad."

The Blacksmith House

The best array of hors d'ouevres and Viennese desserts in Beantown.

WASHINGTON, D.C.

Ridgewell's Caterers

Their gaudy purple trucks can be seen parked in front of all the best addresses. $50 per, average. (They allow you to sample in their kitchen before they deliver.)

Gourmetisserie

Small dinners and parties with a personal touch. Japanese chicken, moussaka, and other exotica.

Willie Mae Carter

She goes it alone (with her own help). A favorite in Washington circles.

Susie Jones

Susie is another favorite for the smaller affairs. If you can't get Willie Mae, you get Susie.

PALM BEACH

Frank Dale

Frank calls himself a "floating" butler and caterer. The ladies love him, so he's booked a year in advance.

The Palm Beach Catering Service

For those who don't have enough foresight or clout to corner Frank Dale. PBCS will do a smash-up job. They come with butlers, musicians, and loads of flowers as well.

CHICAGO

George Jewell

Very elaborate. Extremely grand. High to moderately expensive.

Ingrid Kostrubala

Ingrid's Scandinavian and does things right. If one wants beef, she'll roast the whole steer tenderloin herself. She also makes her own bread and butter.

Gaper's

Weddings, bar mitzvahs, you name it. Very lush, very loud, and very expensive, but a favorite of Chicago's rich folk.

DALLAS

Party Service

Ann and Jim Draper specialize in coming-out parties. They'll mail the invitations, too.

Wall's Catering Service

Bonnie Wall is the person to call for those fabulous (and expensive) weddings.

Aspon's English Bakery

They supply the Dallas upper classes with local specialties: Texas pecan cake, Dobos torte, and pink champagne cake.

SAN FRANCISCO

Tout De Suite Catering

Thomas Thomasser,
butler of the late
Templeton Crocker,
oversees all operations
for the favorites of the
Telegraph Hill crowd.

London Nossman

Ranks second to none.
Considered by many to
be the best—anywhere!
But *very* expensive.

LOS ANGELES

Margaret Paone

Margaret specializes in
"casserole type" fare that
can be eaten "without
too much bother" on the
hoof. Big with
Hollywood party givers.

Mrs. Dickey Catering

Big with Hollywood
party *goers*. The best, so
they say, and more
formal.

Bagatelle

André Pister freezes
everything (including the
pâté en croute). It's all
ready to be popped in
the oven. The really chic
serve it right from the
individual tins.

VII The Rich (Sob!) and the Young Rich

(Or . . . As the Twig Is Bent . . .)

If there are any tears to be shed for the rich, save them for the young. For the junior denizens of "the golden ghetto" are really in bad trouble!

Besides being virtually *persona non grata* at most traditional prep schools and Ivy League colleges these days—due to a traumatic reemphasis on academic accomplishment over bloodlines as a qualification for admission, most of the young, young scions reportedly suffer from a mental aberration known as "dysgradia."

Dysgradia (a quasi-medical term used to describe a disorder in the normal progression of emotional development) is a term coined by a psychiatrist, Burton Wixen, who treated hundreds of rich young people with identical psychological problems before he realized that their "hangups," curiously, resembled the neuroses of another minority: the very poor.

Dr. Wixen is obviously not alone in this opinion. But unlike economic deprivation, spoilation of the rich has taken a long time to be considered a serious mental problem.

In 1976 Dr. Robert Coles, a child psychiatrist on the staff at Harvard who previously wrote solely about the poor and working classes, published a study of children of the very rich, in which he recorded the developing sense of class and money consciousness that occurs among affluent kids at a very early age.

Like an encephalograph, Dr. Coles noted every wave that the knowledge of immense wealth seemed to wreak on a child's brain.

"The rich person's sense of entitlement that begins early on," he observed, "is mind-boggling!"

Too many choices produce a confusion in some children. Indulgence can lead to finickiness. A child who travels from home to home and country to country can easily acquire a sense of instability, a rootlessness not far removed from migratory workers' children.

Rich youngsters (who live in enormous houses) actually

become afraid of their environment and refuse to enter certain rooms, arbitrarily. Though these children are taught manners and know all about playing their roles in the household, they often are isolated and aloof in their relations with subordinates.

Some rich children even sense the weightiness of their position in the world. At school they mistrust fellow students and will become skeptical of a teacher's praise, suspecting that authorities defer to them because of their parents' status.

One ten-year-old told Dr. Coles:

"The principal has to be more careful [with me] than anyone else. When Daddy sends a check, he always gets a nice letter back—he's shown it to me—and the principal says nice things about me. But I only half believe them. He has to say nice things when he's getting hundreds of dollars—thousands, I think."

As the privileged kid grows older, Dr. Coles said, he becomes increasingly aware that he is special, that the world at large respects his parents and is often awed by them. He learns early on about money and the stature it implies. In contrast— even if a poor or working-class child has a background of family love and security—he cannot help but know, as he grows older, the contempt that society has for his background.

Comparing a poor child's visit to the welfare office with the privileged child's trip to meet his trust officer or have lunch at the bank, Dr. Coles concludes:

"It is an event in the lives of both children. They are being educated, told what their existence is all about. One child is learning about the family's dependency and how rude and condescending one's treatment can be; the other learns about the sway of personal power. One learns entitlement, and the other learns vulnerability."

And that's the way it is!

Another psychoanalyst, Dr. Roy R. Grinker, who has a healthy practice among the moneyed of Chicago, believes class differences *can* be over-simplified.

Although Dr. Grinker agrees that unhappiness among the poor often leads to crime and public disapproval while unhappiness among the rich is still universally envied, he claims that the wealthy have a harder time surviving, in the long run.

Patients who come to me . . . are often severely handicapped in
their perception of reality and their ability to deal with it.
Grandiose, hypochondriacal, and exhibitionistic, they have a very
limited awareness of themselves or others. They tend to be self-
centered and easily angered. They lack a capacity for tenderness.
They have failed at most things, so they tend to be indecisive.
They cannot tolerate frustration. They engage in sex compul-
sively, without any real interest in the partner. They have few
interests other than beautiful people . . . or cars . . . or clothes.
They tend to see all the world as either good or bad. Only those
as rich as themselves, they are convinced, are fun to be with.
They believe that only by traveling with the "right people" to the
"right places" can they relieve their frustrations!

A curious fact about Dr. Grinker's revelation is that almost
all of his patients are very young: the average age is well below
30. As the noted critic, Harriet Van Horne observed, when she
read his case histories:
"Let's not have them for dinner, shall we?"
One young girl who became a patient of Dr. Grinker as
part of a probation program after a minor drug arrest, was
particularly uncooperative.
"She saw me as an obligation," the doctor states, "like
walking her dog, which she did rarely and also with great
reluctance."
This patient tried not talking to the doctor at all. Withdrawn for long stretches of her therapy sessions, she finally
broke her silence at Christmastime. Here is the significant
memory of her upper-class childhood, revealing the entire
dysgradia malaise:
Every Christmas this young heiress's grandparents would
place several paper bags containing from $500 to $1,000 in coins
on the dining room table. There was one bag for every grandchild, but each kid had to guess the right amount of coins in a
tote to be able to claim it! Just like a TV giveaway show! The
moppet who came closest to guessing the correct number got the
prize package plus *a bonus yuletide offering* of an extra $1,000
for squandering any (unsupervised) way he saw fit!
Dr. Grinker does not reveal it but one assumes from the
tale that this unhappy girl patient was *one* grandchild who was

not a big winner in the family Christmas lottery. And so the case histories pile up!

Having "the crazies" from time-to-time is not an exclusively *young* rich preoccupation, but it is startling how many cases of "nervous breakdown" and "emotional collapse" are logged among super-rich kids. About 45 percent of all the mental entries noted at private institutions in New York State from 1972 to 1976, according to the National Council on Mental Health, were young men and women between the ages of 18 and 25. All of the entries, what is more significant, came from families listed in the *high* income bracket, and many came from families worth millions. This leads one to the conclusion that neurosis is just another rich inheritance, a bequest not too dissimilar from the responsibility of receiving a dozen ancestral Rembrandts or a block of U.S. Steel.

"One learns to live with it," one young post-debutante of my acquaintance said, unsmilingly, as she booked herself into the Payne Whitney Clinic at New York Hospital for her yearly bout with the psychiatrists. "But thanks to Papa, I will always be able to afford it!"

There is a wonderful story about the rich childhood of Countess Gladys Széchńyi, a former Vanderbilt—and the last of that famous name to occupy The Breakers at Newport (the most elaborate beach cottage ever built in the world, costing about $5 million in a time when a million, as Cleveland Amory puts it, was really a million, and absolutely not to be duplicated today for at least six times as much money).

The late Countess, long Newport's charming doyenne, recalled in her seventies that when she was a child she would often sit behind the ornamental wrought-iron gates that surrounded The Breakers for hours just to overhear the remarks of the cab drivers who took sightseers around to view the majesty.

"Those drivers used to proclaim with awe," said the Countess, sadly, "that it takes four footmen just to open the two sets of double doors—and they eat ice cream inside every day! Today, footmen have disappeared entirely, and everybody has ice cream every day. But are people any happier? Today your child wants to be like your chauffeur's child more than your chauffeur's child wants to be like yours. But is that any better?"

The answer, obviously, was *no* for Countess Széchnyi. But a large segment of her class (equally rich, but younger inheritors) would disagree. Reluctantly wealthy, a brace of independent Boston activists have formed The Haymarket People's Fund to support radical groups involved with "political organizing." Or, as one of the donors simplified it, "Getting people to see that their interests are the same as those of their neighbors."

The idea for "Hay," as it is referred to in rich, young Massachusetts circles, originated with George Pillsbury (heir to the baking fortune of the same name). Mr. Pillsbury, 30, who was active in the anti-war movement at college, says he and his friends wanted to do something with their money "besides giving it to the Red Cross!"

Started in Cambridge a few years ago, Haymarket provides wealthy young people (such as the heirs to fortunes from Sears Roebuck, du Pont, and I.B.M.) with a means of placing their unearned profits in the hands of community groups that are working toward social goals that they believe in.

Many of the donors (who are mostly 30 and under) are chagrined to be connected to family resources.

"Having money makes you different from your friends," explained young Pillsbury. "You don't have to have a job, for one thing. And you have to explain why you're the only one in the crowd with a tan. It makes you feel guilty!"

One alternative would appear to be: run with your own crowd. But Haymarket donors eschew dumb rich kids along with unearned chattels. *Embarras de richesses,* the French would call it. Those groups that "Hay" has financed in the past two and one-half years (in the New England area only) include radical community newspapers, tenants' unions, an activist organization opposing nuclear power, and, oddly enough, a bunch of freelance woodcutters in rural Maine, who are trying to become unionized. If it's a good cause, let the chips fall where they may!

While Haymarket flourishes exclusively in the Cambridge

area, its ingrown, anti-capitalist attitude recently extended itself to a secret enclave at Woolman Hill (a Quaker retreat in South Deerfield, Massachusetts), where a *sub rosa* conference was held among 30 or 40 of the sons and daughters of the richest people in America.

The conference of October, 1977 (held under maximum security lest a kidnapping attempt result from any media coverage), was the third in a series held all over the United States designed to instruct rich kids on how to cope with their problems. The first dealt with interpersonal relationships: how to contend with less rich friends and lovers, etc. The second engaged in the technicalities of prosperity: how to take control of your wealth; setting up wills; and dealings with trust officers! The conference at Woolman Hill, on the other hand, was more specific: how to give your windfall away was the theme.

"It's really important for people who have inherited vast fortunes to encourage others that it is no sin to spread it around," one of the participants declared somewhat loftily. "Most rich kids are in the closet. They're embarrassed, conflicted, and confused about their money. This session tried to get them 'out of the woodwork' and into the specious [sic] halls of social conscience!"

"Specious" is apparently the salient word in that disclosure. A caveat to the young-rich conference appeared in New York's *Village Voice* some weeks after the event—and offered what some consider a simpler solution to the problem.

"If *they* would invest only a mite of the accrued interest from their holdings in a lobby for tax reform," the newspaper advised, "these rich kids and their successors would not have any money to get rid of—for it would all go to the government!"

Even the stuffy young-rich—who continue to *like* their family funds—are not exactly immune to the problems that lie beyond the nursery and faithful nanny in her blue cape and starched moral fiber. In a shattering piece of editorial scare tactics, *Town & Country* magazine revealed not long ago that it is becoming harder than ever to enroll fair-haired inheritors into the "rightest" and oldest Ivy League schools.

The reasons are manifold, but in the words of Keith David,

dean of undergraduate admissions at Yale, "Colleges today focus on academically talented people rather than social or cash register names."

The biggest change in admissions at Harvard, Yale, and Princeton in the past decade has been the sharp increase in women applicants and the acceptance of students from "culturally underprivileged backgrounds" who demonstrate capabilities and a sense of initiative that make their selection unquestionable. There is no longer any one "right" name that automatically opens the school door. And as one Ivy League admissions director declared (after requesting anonymity, of course):

"I can remember when the quota here referred to the number of Jews or (God forbid) blacks we accepted to keep a point ahead of outright discrimination. Now, in the educational turn-around of the '70s, 'quota' applies to the minimum of something less than whiz kids: the amount of young Mellons, Rockefellers, and Whitneys we can accept without entirely losing our academic standing!"

Another blow to "undemocratic education" was struck some while back when "prep schools" (even the toniest of them) became a middle-class milieu. For generations these establishments had been considered the bastions of privilege, cloistered classrooms and campuses whose playing fields were reserved exclusively for the sons and daughters of social somebodies. And, like the Hamptons, they were considered permanently off-limits to the *nouveau riche,* the non-Christian, and the nondescript.

What happened?

A decade ago applications to the best schools dropped off, sharply. Such institutions, it was bruited about loudly, were simply too expensive for inflation-pressed parents (even rich ones) to afford comfortably. Besides, in the cultural upheaval of the mid '60s "preppie-attitudes were still so elitist," said their critics, "that the system would shortly be dispensed with by social revolution, anyway!"

The doomsayers were slightly premature, however. Faced with economic annihilation, the best schools took the second best solution: they went democratic. And their enrollment (no longer homogeneously white or wealthy) quadrupled in five years.

Why did the middle class want in? Well, it was not for academia alone, according to the educators. Although most parents of enrolled prep-school attendees seem to believe their youngsters were short-changed in public schools, something other than a simon-pure education motive is at stake here. Particularly when one considers that tuition at most private schools hovers inexorably at about $5,000.

"Glamour," says the headmaster at one of the best prep schools in the country, "is the answer! Having a kid *here* makes the bourgeois feel like a patrician—every time around."

But how does it make the *patrician* feel?

Not good!

Time was, when Dink Stover was doing and dying on the playing fields of Lawrenceville, one could be certain of a few verities. Attendance at the right prep school combined with the right pedigree always meant acceptance at Yale (or Princeton or Harvard, for that matter). But not any more. There are just too many who want *in!* Phillips Academy of Andover, Massachusetts, one of the country's oldest and most prestigious private schools, received 2,300 applications for 380 vacancies in 1977. The Taft School of Watertown, Connecticut, reported over 7 applications for each available place, and even venerable Groton (alma mater of Franklin D. Roosevelt) received over 500 applications for just 95 places among last year's student body.

Middle-class rich elders are so plagued by the problem of "where to put the kids" that they automatically register them with sterling prep schools at birth. A small minority has even taken to shipping their progeny abroad (in a reverse-snob foreign invasion) for the proper touch of class.

An abbreviated listing of the good-better-best schools follows. Each is starred in order of desirability by the rich, with three stars indicating most coveted.

CO-ED SCHOOLS

*** *St. Paul's School*
Concord, New Hampshire
Wolcotts, Wheelers, Vanderbilts, Ingersolls, Biddles, Lindsays, and Pillsburys. Need one say more?

*** *St. Mark's School*
Southborough, Massachusetts
Loaded with Cabots and Adamses. The favorite of the Boston set.

*** *Groton*
Groton, Massachusetts
One of the most eminent, J. P. Morgan was a founding father. Auchincloss and Roosevelt are household names.

*** *Phillips Academy*
Andover, Massachusetts
"Andover" has its share of Bostonians, but the main attraction seems to be the Abbot Academy next door. According to the boys of Andover, the prettiest girls go there.

*** *The Taft School*
Watertown, Connecticut
Founded by President Taft's brother, Horace. Students write "pledge" at the head of each test paper—their way of saying they haven't cheated.

*** *Choate School*
Wallingford, Connecticut
A pioneer in the education field; considered by many to be *the* best. It boasts a JFK Library (he was a graduate) and has an abundance of Kennedys and Vanderbilts.

** *Phillips Exeter*
Exeter, New Hampshire
The choice of the Fish and Gardner families. Philosophy and politics play a big part here, so "society" gives it a second-class rating.

***St. George's School*
Newport, Rhode Island
Founded by John Nicholas Brown (whose

family also founded Brown U.), St. George's sits on a cliff above the breakers. The headmaster's dogs run free (including class rooms). No wonder Pell kids love it.

** *Middlesex School*
Concord, Massachusetts

The Lowells and Forbeses send their kids here. Most famous for coining the "St. Grottlesex" cognomen, which applies to all "New England type" schools.

* *Hotchkiss School*
Lakeville, Connecticut

Founded by the widow of the man who "perfected" the machine gun, Hotchkiss is a favorite of the Midwest set: Armours, Buchanans, Fields, Fords, Swifts.

* *Kent School*
Kent, Connecticut

Kent was one of the first to go co-ed—except for the libraries. There is still one for the boys and one for the girls.

* *Putney School*
Putney, Vermont

For rich intellects only. Society frowns on the liberal (sometimes radical) views of the faculty. The kids even have to make their own beds *and* clean the bathrooms.

BOYS' SCHOOLS

*** *Deerfield Academy*
Deerfield, Massachusetts

Historic Deerfield, founded 1792, is the "only" place (socially) for those who want to separate the boys from the girls.

*** *The Lawrenceville School*
Lawrenceville, New Jersey

The English "master" system was introduced to the U.S. here. A favorite for Princeton-bound boys.

** *Avon Old Farms School*
Avon, Connecticut

The most beautiful of all, the place is virtually a museum. (Valuable antiques adorn every room.) Once scorned as frivolous, it's gaining ground academically.

* *The Hill School*
Pottstown, Pennsylvania

The academic goals center around

"intellectual freedom," provided one can get past the incredible soot that constantly envelopes Pottstown.

* *Robert Louis Stevenson*
Pebble Beach, California

A West Coast favorite. Lots of Hollywood children.

GIRLS' SCHOOLS

*** *The Ethel Walker School*
Simsbury, Connecticut

The "right" school for all the "right" people.

*** *The Emma Willard School*
Troy, New York

Troy is not the prettiest town in the world, but the standards are the best.

** *Chatham Hall*
Chatham, Virginia

The "only" place for any upright Southern debutante.

* *Foxhollow School*
Lenox, Massachusetts

Strictly for the "proper" Bostonians.

* *Foxcroft School*
Middleburg, Virginia

Horsey, horsey, horsey!

* *Miss Porter's School*
Farmington, Connecticut

Where Jackie O. went. Due to the worst scandal in private school history, Miss Porter's has lost its three-star rating.

* *The Madeira School*
Greenway, Virginia

For those Southern debutantes who can't make it into Chatham Hall.

ENGLISH BOARDING SCHOOLS
FOR BOYS

*** *Winchester College*
Winchester, Hampshire

Like most English schools, very difficult to enter, but some Americans do get in, usually for the last year. The child must be registered on his eighth birthday and is not admitted before he is 12. Once chosen, he must take a very difficult exam. The effort is worth it, though; 70 percent of its graduates go on to Oxford or Cambridge.

*** *Eton College*
Windsor, Berkshire

Traditional school of the wealthy and noble families of England. Hence, a social credential much sought after. Eton does admit students from all over the world, but only the most esteemed names are found in Eton's 400-year-old halls. Little bluebloods must be registered at birth or shortly thereafter.

*** *Harrow School*
Harrow on the Hill, Middlesex

Like Eton, boys must be registered at birth. Also like Eton, Harrow is popular with the wealthy and social classes. Started in 1608, it rests on 300 "hilltop" acres, half of which is a working dairy farm.

*** *Rugby School*
Rugby, Warwickshire

Another excellent school with a high adademic rating. About half go on to Cambridge or Oxford.

** *Westminster School*
Westminster, London

Again, the boys are registered at birth, interviewed and tested 3 years prior to entrance. Located in the Little Dean's Yard adjoining Westminster Abbey, tots are allowed to wander the streets of London off hours.

FOR GIRLS

*** *Heathfield School*
Ascot, Berkshire

Eton's other half; for the daughters of the wealthy and noble. It is 35 minutes from London, within easy reach of cultural events required of the young ladies. The social life includes parties with young Etonians at nearby Windsor.

*** *Wycombe Abbey*
High Wycombe, Buckinghamshire

Famed for its high standards. All girls, regardless of faith, must attend daily vespers.

*** *Sherborne School for Girls*
Sherborne, Dorset

Science and music emphasized here. The school has 2 orchestras and a chamber ensemble plus a 60-voice choir. Academic achievement is high, with many girls going on to Oxford, Cambridge, and medical schools.

** *St. Mary's Convent*
Ascot, Berkshire

One of the prettiest, they say that it is unlikely that any girl can come away from St. Mary's without an appreciation of beauty. Princess Caroline of Monaco did her stint here.

SWISS SCHOOLS

*** *Villa Brillantmont*
Lausanne

Famous for its "ultra-exclusive" policies. English-speaking students are a rarity.

*** *Institut Videmanette*
Rougemont

Near Gstaad, it's a favorite of the English and Americans, who make up 25 percent of its total enrollment.

** *St. George's*
Montreaux

Actually an English boarding school, St. George's is a favorite of American executives living abroad.

Le Rosey
Lac Leman

One of the most expensive; recently co-ed. Loaded with the children of modern-day tycoons.

Even a really *good* school is no assurance that your rich, young stripling will grow into a hardy oak some day—but the odds so far seem to favor "Establishment education" as a firmer prerequisite for maturation than so-called "progressive" halls of learning.

One rule of thumb for rich parents: Don't send your kids to California schools! Remember that when the SLA kidnapped her—and permanently placed her graven image in the rogues' gallery of the world—Patty Hearst was studying art (and heaven knows what else) at the University of California at Berkeley.

Ever hear about Blue Sunshine? You would if you'd been an undergrad at Stanford a while back. This is no Hawaiian rock group but a full-fledged LSD derivative, at one time imbibed by rich kids on that campus; and it still is producing one helluva side effect ten years later. According to the Federal Drug Enforcement Agency, the intake of Blue Sunshine at Stanford has caused myriad cases of hair loss, paranoid tendencies, and (in some cases) severe homicidal impulses. Strike two!

J. Paul Getty III, a U.C.L.A. dropout and grandson of the late oil magnate, was declared incapable of managing his own money in Los Angeles late last year. Though he is married and the father of a small son, young Mr. Getty agreed to a court request in which his maternal grandfather, Judge George Harris of the U.S. District Court of San Francisco, told the court that he was financially improvident, easily victimized, and in danger of going broke. In his own defense, Mr. Getty stated that "I managed the best way I could. After all, I *was* a business administration major." California, you're out! As a molder of our nation's youth, at least.

Not that the eastern educational establishment is without some blemish either, these days.

A motto hanging high over the doorway to Miss Porter's School in Farmington, Connecticut, for almost a century and a half proudly proclaims a Latin legend to the world: *"Puellae venerunt, Abigrunt mulieres"* (Girls they enter, Women they leave). And generations of well-to-do mamas and papas never doubted the translation for an instant.

Certainly hundreds of well-bred alumnae (such as Jacqueline Bouvier Kennedy Onassis) proved the point ten times over, assuming their allotted places in society with a deep bow toward their grateful alma mater. And, though etiquette classes and social dancing have long since been excised from the school's curriculum, today's parents still send their daughters off with the expectation that the girls will be well-educated, suitably chaperoned, and somewhat sheltered from the X-rated world outside.

Late in 1976, however, Farmington lost its hallowed reputation. The fall came about through a lacerating human tragedy. A pregnant 14-year-old sophomore (in her first year at the school) apparently delivered herself of a child in the girls' dormitory, then wrapped the baby in a plastic bag and hid it under a bed. The infant was reported to be dead when it was discovered, the police were summoned, and the worst scandal in private-school history ensued.

Shocked school officials sent the errant student home— where she was quietly hospitalized. The case later was referred to the state's Juvenile Court, where, according to Robert Ertl, the director of probation in Hartford, "It was investigated to determine whether there was criminal negligence involved in the death."

Apparently there was not. Several months later, the chief medical examiner's report vindicated the girl of any wrongdoing, and the case was dismissed. The case against Miss Porter's School, however, still goes on in the minds of many potential students and parents, who, rightly or wrongly, adjudge the institution guilty of gross insensibility to the problems of one of its charges. It is a verdict that Miss Porter's will not easily live down!

Rich kids today do live in a changing world, and that is the biggest part of their problem.

"Your generation—rich or poor—knew where you belonged," said Thomas Chase Phipps III recently, as he considered the possibility of leaving Dartmouth (after his junior term) to become a chef.

"Mine, on the other hand, smokes a lot of grass and hasn't the faintest clue what side to join!"

Things may be looking up for young (and rich) Mr.

Phipps's generation, however. When Yale's crew of service workers recently called a strike for higher pay and went off the job (of cleaning and tidying the hallowed halls), over 4,800 undergraduates crossed their picket lines—to make beds, dust, and vacuum the living quarters and generally do the necessary tasks (such as cleaning the toilets) that keep a dormitory dazzling!

Less *noblesse* and more *oblige* is the name of that touch of democracy. And, hold on, a recent society-page report noted that many (really well-born) young women these days look on the debut as mere ritual and consider that the money would be better spent on one of the pressing social issues. Nina Rumbough, daughter of Stanley Rumbough, Jr., and Dina Merrill (now Mrs. Cliff Robertson) said *no* a while back, but she did it in a slip-sliding way; at the very last mo, she conceded to a party given by her party-loving grandmother, the late Marjorie Merriweather Post.

Other, more recent holdouts against the deb scene have not budged on the issue at all. Tracy Swope, whose parents are Mr. and Mrs. Bayard Swope, Jr., and Cassandra Skouras, daughter of Mr. and Mrs. Spyros Skouras, Jr., absolutely put their pretty little feet down on the subject.

They are two members of the young rich who know where they belong, Tom!

VIII   How to Live Like the Rich
(Or . . . Where They Stop and Where They Shop)

To indulge in a bit of chic-speak, the most "laid back" group characteristic of the very rich is their restiveness. What the right people have in common is an attention span that would rival Doctor Mendel's fruit fly.

Claiming the prerogative of discoverers, they spend most of their lives ferreting out what is new, untried, and untrod on the fashion landscape, dress designers and discothèques by turn. For apparent patronage at these fledgling nests of enterprise (though often they pay nothing at all for commodities received) can create instant success for any establishment—and they know it.

The rich, however, are not entirely generous with their endorsement; they require peer exclusivity in return for their bestowal of sanction. And once a service to which they have subscribed gains too much press acknowledgment or too much public (sub-order) acceptance, they desert the cause.

Like winged creatures, these dispensers of fame and fortune are impelled to flit from couturier to couturier, caterer to caterer, and cultural explosion to cultural explosion in a mad exercise of options. They must be the initiators of fashion—or wither and die!

Most apparent to social birdwatchers, like myself, is the rigid code of what is "in" and what is "out" (for these super-rich) at any given moment in their lives. The current attitude toward being *seen* abroad is worth noting here:

No one in the rarefied flock of flighty tastemakers—whose exploits we follow so vicariously from over Suzy's and Eugenia's shoulders—will be seen *out* on Saturday nights any more. For Saturday night is dead, *de trop* and absolutely unthinkable for any social function whatsoever these days.

That is not to imply that restaurants, theaters, and night spots aren't jam-packed on Saturday nights anymore—because they are. But they are precisely packed with *arrivistes* and out-of-towners; the kind of crush the "right" people stay at home to avoid.

In times gone by the right people, who no longer venture

121

forth on a Saturday evening, would rather have succumbed to Spanish influenza than admit they were simply at liberty. Staying home was anathema to the restless breed of those early rich. (That is how they earned all the sobriquets for their eventful past: the Gilded Age, Café Society, the Jet-Set, and even the Beautiful People.) The lust of those adventuresome types was to go everywhere: to be seen, admired, and even envied. Now, however, the rich stay at home, for Saturday night is no longer a chic time to be seen anywhere.

The condition of the chic evening out has become so dolorous of late that John Corry, a reporter who writes for the *New York Times,* appraised the situation last year.

"While Saturday night is not chic at all, Monday, Wednesday, and Friday nights are not much, either. Tuesday and Thursday nights *are* chic; Sunday night is, too. But Saturday is out, probably forever."

Corry reasons that the root of Saturday's decline is obvious—and mostly has to do with territorial imperatives. Chic people have a tendency to hang out solely with other chic people, which is how they define their existence and in a sense know that they are truly chic themselves.

While this kind of inbred socialism is fairly harmless, it is, nevertheless, decidedly restrictive. There is no place that the "right people" (in New York, at least) can possibly wander off to on a Saturday evening and still be assured that they will find a minimum sampling of class equals. This kind of inhibitory factoring might force television ratings up on Saturday nights, but it is certainly hell on the social life!

The only alternative to enforced "at-homes" is to be invited out to some other "right" person's house; but the law of diminishing returns precludes any rush of hospitality these days.

For the truly chic, there are only three nights to be errant. Sunday is a very good night to go on the town, and it is even better augury when one is invited to someone's home for an informal dinner party on the first night of the week. Have Corry's words on the subject:

"No one knows why chic people started having informal dinners on Sunday, but many chic people do. Moreover, Sunday night is the only night the truly chic will go to Pearl's Chinese restaurant on West 48th Street. If a truly chic person invites you to dinner at Pearl's, you will be invited *only* for a Sunday night. No one knows why. . . .

"Monday nights are neuters . . . even though they were once black-tie nights at the opera. Before that, in fact, they were white tie. Now Mondays are mostly for benefit performances and charity balls. That is because business is slow in theaters, and hotel banquet rooms and managements are inclined to hustle up extra business by giving charity organizations a break on the prices. Otherwise, Monday night has nothing to recommend it.

"Tuesday is different," Corry continues. "Tuesday is chic . . . almost by default. It is a big night for backgammon in New York, and backgammon is very chic. Also the Algonquin Round Table once met on Tuesday nights, and although the Round Table is dead, its cachet lingers on. Mostly, however, Tuesday night is chic for no reason at all."

Thursday, we are informed, is chic for several reasons, the most traditional and the oldest being the singular fact that Thursday night was the maid's night off. Chic people had no alternative to this *impasse*—except to eat out, on the town. Otherwise, they probably didn't eat at all. The tradition survives at such deluxe dining rooms as "21" or Grenouille, and now Mortimers; they get more celebrated folk per capita on Thursday than on any other night of the week. Thursday is, of course, still the chic night of the week for an important dinner party, although it is always expected that guests will have gone cocktail-partying beforehand. So the chic Thursday dinner never begins before nine. Mr. Corry stated most equivocally that: "The most chic time of the week is between 10:45 and 11:00 P.M. on Thursday. For that is when guests arise from dinner tables all over the East Side and say that they must leave early because they have to catch a plane for North Africa or California or go to the Bahamas or be on the "Today" show on Friday morning. There is nothing more chic than that.

*   *   *

Undeniably, the rich are a fad-prone clique with no allegiance whatsoever to yesterday's passing fancies. The early sixties saw their renascent devotion to two sports that had been considered a middle-class dominion since the turn of the century: football and tennis.

For the elite, football was considered a purely parochial social event like alumni reunions. Old Ivy Leaguers met on the fields of Harvard, Princeton, Yale, and Dartmouth and shared the embarrassment of defeat and victory along with their nostalgia. But professional football was decidedly a proletarian diversion—and the rich shunned it, along with baseball, basketball, and hockey.

The change in attitude toward "pro-sports" is always linked to the inauguration of John F. Kennedy, when the familial conceit of touch football games and an emphasis on physical fitness in general entered the upper-class consciousness. The rich, suffused by the aura of those Golden Boys at play behind the White House, began seriously to support and even acquire professional football teams of their own. To legitimatize the contest!

In the end their patronage was short-lived. As football stadiums filled with upwardly mobile middle-class fans (with no reluctance to spend $10 to $12 for seats), the rich attendance diminished. And the "right" people deserted football once again.

Tennis has had an even chancier fate. The favored pastime of the very wealthy from the turn of the century until the Depression, the sport lost its following after World War II, when the governmental tax bite ate up most of the grander manor houses that could afford maintaining private courts.

The tennis revival generally is credited to the athletic and sexual prowess of one Pancho Gonzalez. This extraordinary Mexican champion's reputation for service among the beautiful socialites of the Hamptons became so fabled and well-chronicled during the mid-sixties that a cult of less-than-lionizing sportsmen formed the Hampton Bath and Tennis Club in self-defense, attempting to stem his lead both on the courts and between the sheets.

Though that is only a rumor, tennis did, in fact, make its

return to popularity on the South Fork of Long Island. Between 1965 and 1969 it became the only game in town, completely outstripping squash and golf, which some while before had overtaken swimming and croquet.

Tennis's vogue (among the rich, at least) was *fini* by 1970, when it was replaced by an excessive interest in horses. And though the original fad produced only a minor rush of court construction in East Hampton and Brookville, it has permanently changed the habits of the middle class, who carry their racquets instead of attaché cases to the office on Mondays, Wednesdays, and Fridays, which are the most popular days in semi-rich circles.

Aside from sports, the main preoccupation of the rich for the past half-dozen years has been psychoanalysis. Psychological chichi first budded in the early '30s when the mere descriptive term "Freudian" cast an aura of unmistakable vogue on any form of outré behavior to which it was applied. Nonetheless, psychiatry as a fashion did not come to full-flowering until the late '40s and '50s when the "right" people had the option of Horneyian, Jungian, Adlerian, or Sullivanian therapies to unravel their mental wool.

However, when the rising middle class appropriated the same neuroses in the '60s, the rich quickly recovered and psychiatry was out!

Some claim the recent revival of interest in psychotherapy returned with the economic recession of 1972, when the strapped middle class was forced to eschew the luxury. Others state that the mental woes of the rich surfaced with their class disappointment in Nixon. (There are two popular theories on this subject.)

At the close of 1977, John Leonard, chief cultural correspondent for the *New York Times,* stated flatly that:

"Analysis for the moment seems to be out of fashion in New York. In fashion are horses and the ballet."

To such a catalog of cosmic *comme il faut,* add "water," too!

Water-chic arose with the revival of psychiatry, but there is no appreciable diminishment in sight. From the beginning of the '70s there has been an inordinate rich preoccupation with bidets, saunas, Jacuzzis, and, most recently, indoor swimming pools.

In spite of threatened utility hikes and the built-in hazard of vertical fabrication, most of these installations are proliferating in big cities. And no penthouse, brownstone, or duplex cooperative is considered truly livable these days without some form of private irrigation on the premises.

"After a Rolls Royce, complete with liveried chauffeur and a low license number, what else could be the ultimate status symbol than a private swimming pool in your own city residence!"

Thus posits a provocative piece in the same issue of the paper that registered the demise of analysis on the social scale.

H_2O is obviously cleaner, if not cheaper, in the long run! The most talked of pool about town (in a plethora of watery circumjacencies) is a prime swimming hole currently being installed between the 46th and 47th floors of the prestigious Olympic Tower in New York. The apartment itself cost about $400,000; the swimming pool (of fiberglass-coated steel plate) is costing its new tenant (at this writing) $70,000 without installation. The pool will measure about 15 by 20 feet, the local scuttlebutt reports, and it is described as something slightly larger than a big, big bathtub.

There was a curious epithet abroad when I was growing up, newly *pauvre,* that stated: "Soak the rich!" And while I never fully understood the emotional context of the aphorism, I have long been in sympathy with the doctrine. Mr. Adnan Khashoggi, the Saudi Arabian millionaire who shortly will be swimming his forty laps east of the RCA tower, *deserves* the bath.

Khashoggi, an OPEC industrialist, is said to maintain residences in London, Paris, and two Saudi cities, among which the Olympic Tower is the least prepossessing, poolwise!

In New York, where one can spend $10,000, $20,000, or as much as half a million for an ablution tailored to a specific requirement, Ronald Brandenburg of the Land Distributing Corporation, a pool servicing company in Brooklyn, recently declared:

"There is no limit to the cost—if you are talking about a pool 10 or 20 stories up in Manhattan. But the better known distributors won't even set foot on those jobs. If something that high were to spring a leak, y'know, it could destroy a whole building!"

Oil magnates do not worry about piddling problems like that. Neither do assorted privileged owners of other private reservoirs, apparently. In Manhattan's East Side alone there are reputed to be over three hundred such installations at the present time—at an averate cost of $30,000.

Bidets, saunas, and Jacuzzis? We stopped counting.

*   *   *

Truman Capote, that dedicated chronicler of the foibles of the high and mighty, recently summed up the difference between the rich and, well, you and me. "Vegetables," he announced.

Vegetables?

"Vegetables!" Capote reaffirmed. "At [the late] Babe Paley's table or Bunny Mellon's or Betsy Whitney's or C-Z's, haven't you ever noticed how extraordinary the vegetables are? The smallest, most succulent peas, lettuce, the most delicate baby corn, asparagus, limas the size of cuticles . . . everything so fresh, almost unborn. That's what you can do when you have an acre or so of greenhouses."

Mrs. Diana Vreeland, with her accustomed panache, publicly hailed Capote's view as a stunning piece of social observation.

Much as I admire their twin authority on the subject, as an ex-caterer, I must respectfully dissent. The vegetables at most of the better tables I observed were more often than not waterlogged, frozen, or canned. Canned vegetables most frequently make an appearance when the food is prepared at home by a permanent kitchen staff and the lady of the house does her own shopping. (Rich women inevitably market for their households out of paranoia. If this chore were entrusted to their domestics, they fear, the servants would rob them blind.)

The rich, as a whole, maintain an idiosyncratic sort of provender. Their refrigerators are of a necessity bare—so there will be room for the bought-goods that the inevitable troupe of caterers bring with them. (Leftovers are the prerogative of these same food entrepreneurs, so there is usually little of yesterday's repast, at any event.) Flowers usually sit in the richest refrigerators in town; orchids never arranged for a centerpiece until the last possible hour to keep them at maximum waxiness.

Dinner party food is sure to be showy, but the dictum is always for a movable feast. Courses are not designed for lingering enjoyment among the upper classes, and the guests of honor are required to be more highly seasoned than most of the food they eat.

Cold salmon in green mayonnaise is a rich-table staple. It is served with such frequency during "the season" however, that Rosemary Kent, the intrepid social reporter, was said to have developed an allergy that turned her a deathly shade of viridian merely on contact with a duly laden buffet table.

Similarly, there has been a beef Wellington rut (and, on a minor scale, a *veau Prince Orloff* rut) among the "right" hostesses that only now (in the earnest period of tight money) is giving way to earlier hard-times standbys such as *boeuf Bourguignonne* and *suprème de Volaille*. Princess Peggy d'Arenberg (the Standard Oil heiress) allowed on occasion that she never varies her menus at dinner parties. Rock Cornish game hen or chicken Kiev were standards on her table because they were absolutely foolproof, she said.

The rich tend to limit their menus to unsurprising dishes at best, but the Princess's poultry fix seems to bespeak something more than mere consuetude—*economy*, to put it bluntly. But then it has been noted that chicken is showing up with alarming regularity everywhere. At Mrs. Ahmet Ertegun's dinner parties for 20, chicken with walnuts (Turkish style, like Mr. Ertegun) often will be the *plat du jour*. And Mrs. Bertrand Taylor III almost never gives a ciné-buffet (for 60 or so friends) where chicken mousse does not appear—between the *salade Niçoise* and the *gravlax*.

Some wag at a recent dinner party (at Mrs. Donald Stralem's—who unflaggingly serves up stew) reported that since fowl is such an eligible viand these days, knowing Frank Perdue has become as weighty as name-dropping Halston.

When quizzed on the subject, Stephen Birmingham said:

"The rich appear to eat little, but it is not simply because of a desire to stay thin. They believe that eating a lot or setting out a lavish meal is a bit vulgar."

Mr. Birmingham is of the opinion that the rich live by a rather archaic Puritan ethic when it comes to indulgences. They regard eating extravagantly on the same level as consorting with call girls, catering to baser instincts, as it were. A long-time watchdog of the rich, Birmingham believes that the moneyed tend not to buy or serve expensive foods because they are at a loss to enjoy them. For the upper classes, eating is nothing more than a dreary necessity. One must eat—so they do it. For no one, alas, can survive on gin and tonic, alone!

Mr. Birmingham is a keen sociologist. "If you study the buffet tables at clubs that the Old Guard rich frequent, you will see exactly what they like to eat: deviled eggs, cocktail onions, smoked oysters on Melba rounds, thick club sandwiches, halves of waterlogged lobsters with Hellmann's mayonnaise, and cold, collapsed, overdone roast beef with rubbery Yorkshire pudding," he points out.

The Old Guard thinks that the food served at their clubs is "super" because it is precisely what they have always been fed at home!

Here is a random sampling of the rich Establishment diet:

Snacking and Dipping Canapés

Crackers are very important to the rich. They spend a great deal of time in the crispy-crunchy departments of the major gourmet groceries, buying everything from Carr's water biscuits to Grielle Toast, Fritos, and potato chips. Mrs. Arthur Stanton, however, never allows any crumbly thing on her cocktail tray except Bremer Wafers.

The rich often have these cocktail crochets: Cristophe de Menil is given to great trays of raw vegetables (color coordinated to match her paintings) while M. Guerrand Hermes serves only wheels of cheese, sans wafers or bread. Most often, rich hostesses do their own hors d'oeuvres for even posh dinner parties—so they can axe the caterer's bill somewhat. What they usually provide are Dilly Beans and bottled Vienna sausages and a dip that is composed of half sour cream and half dehydrated soup mix, just as their counterparts in the hinterlands did twenty years ago.

Soups

Soup is a vital course to the rich because it is part of an entertaining ritual observed from the nursery on. Also, soup sipping is rather like conspicuous consumption since nobody but the truly upper classes has family bowl or bouillon cups of Sèvre or Haviland any more. Usually at contemporary dinner parties, soups are clear and thin. Sometimes they are spiked with California sherry. In summer the rich taste goes creamy: cold vichyssoise or Billi Bi (a mussel and white wine creation that brings to mind glorious memories of Le Pavillion when it is served); the adventurous spoon-up jellied madrilène from the can; and dab-on sour cream and red caviar. The most elegant soup I ever encountered in a rich kitchen was *creme primavera,* a delicate curry-scented cream of fresh peas. Mrs. Marjorie Merriwether Post was the hostess who ladled it forth, but she liked her food more than the rest of her class.

Luncheons

The rich like to eat soft food, preferably the kind that does not require the effort of a fork and knife. Quiche Lorraine, soufflés, and crepes (always with bland upholstery, such as creamed chicken) suit their taste admirably. Essentially they prefer their midday meals to be soothing experiences (with nap afterward).

Dinners

At home, away from the madding crowd, the fare will be very simple and Spartan. Lean chops (never more than one per person) or chicken wings; sometimes a roast lamb—that will reappear as a curry at a small dinner party Sunday next. The rich *are* spare in their indulgences. They never eat potatoes or bread. Although they insist on hard dinner rolls at the table, they seem to enjoy breaking and buttering them more than consuming them.

Vegetables

Peas, canned, frozen, or (rarely) fresh is the hands down, number one rich people's favorite vegetable.

Salad

Often served but usually skipped. Chancy hostesses, schooled in Paris, know it is a necessity as a "digestive," but, frankly, they would prefer not to serve it at all. At rich functions no one usually smokes until after the entree has been consumed, so the salad course usually becomes a retainer for cigarette stubs—and that's not quite nice, after all.

Desserts

The rich have a communal sweet tooth—but they are hard put to be inventive when it comes to a meal's end. Anything soft, sticky, and served over ice cream or sherbert usually will suffice. The intrepid insist on mousse. Dina Merrill Robertson once asked me to produce a peach mousse for 50 at a dinner party she was planning. When she heard the price, however, ($50 for a basin as large as the sinks at the Ritz) she demurred. Too pricey!

The rich do not ever serve what pleases their guests; and the only appetite they ever consider whetting is, obviously, their own. Aristotle Onassis's favorite snack was a trencher of sliced red onions marinated in olive oil with a splash of lemon. Inevitably, that was what his distinguished guests were served for luncheon once they were miles and miles away from shore on the *Christina!*

* * *

In spite of inflation, the age of synthetics, and a dearth of true craftsmanship anywhere, life still can be beautiful for rich shoppers. The secret is knowing where to go, what to expect, and how to demand a discount; the "right" purchaser always rates that automatic privilege.

Jacqueline Onassis, more than any other contemporary in her class, is considered the complete consumer. She has made mercantile interchange into such an art form that even established entrepreneurs, anesthetized by her presence in their emporiums, slash prices outrageously at the merest suggestion of her demurral.

More often than not, it is a wise business decision, too, since the Onassis stamp of approval on a discovery (be it a Bokhara or a brioche) insures instant financial stability for a firm. Wherever she shops, New York, Paris, or even Timbuktu, Mrs. Onassis is obviously *known;* therefore, she never has to pay for her purchases.

Like most of her social peers, she considers the idea of carrying cash cumbersome and checks or credit cards demeaning—so Mrs. Onassis opens charge accounts. At Florentine art galleries, Medina bazaars, or roadside stands she merely says: "I'll take that!" And she does.

The following is a brief compilation of some of the "in" shops and services the "right" people (like Mrs. O.) patronize most frequently these days. But imitative consumers should be forewarned: the rich taste is a capricious one, and today's fad might very well be tomorrow's fadeout!

Where They Buy Their Clothes

Kenzo—Paris

The hottest look in town. His latest take nerve to wear, though; jackets three sizes too large, meant to be worn open, *sans* anything underneath!

Karl Lagerfield (Chloe)—Paris

Billowy blouses, skirts, dresses in "the romantic manner." (Better than nudity," says Karl.)

Sonia Rykiel—Paris

The only place to find sweaters these days.

Yves St. Laurent—Paris
Of course, of course!

St. Laurent (Rive Gauche)—New York
Leftovers from Paris.

Adolfo—New York
By appointment only.
Need one say more?

Thierry Mugler—Paris
The most daring to date.
"Neo-Nazi" chic.
Leather, nail studs,
storm-trooper caps.

Chez Ninon—New York
Gowns start at $4,000.

Halston—New York
Not everyone is
permitted to shop here.
Clients (on a first name
basis) are Ba, C-Z, Liz, etc.

Bijan Pakzad—Beverly Hills
On Rodeo Drive, his
"proper customer" is
"the man who earns
$100,000 a month."

Claude Montana—Paris
Trendy. More S & M
than Mugler.

Menagerie—San Francisco
Privy Paris collections.

I. Magnin—San Francisco
Old Guard
Establishment *cum*
charge accounts, but
backpackers wouldn't be
caught dead. . . .

Bergdorf Goodman—New York
Revived showing of
Paris originals: Dior,
Yves, Givenchy, etc.
Draws the C-Z crowd.

Cassini—New York
Was a Kennedy favorite.
Now losing ground.

Obiko—San Francisco
Small designer couture.
New, chic, and private;
the West Coast rich
would like to keep it
that way!

Giorgio—Beverly Hills
Latest European styles.
The typical Rodeo Drive
shopper can spend
$30,000 in two hours.

Courreges—New York
French masters off-the-
rack. But tacky
management, so CCs
stay off-limits.

134

Dior Boutique—Paris
It's neither "in" nor really chic any more—but it's still a habit, obviously.

Jean Claude de Luca—Paris
New to the swim. His designs use vast amounts of fabric—so wearers appear "gaunt" by comparison.

Roger Vivier—Paris
The only shoes in the whole world.

Valentino—New York
Not for serious spending . . . but. . . .

Martha—Palm Beach
The Queen of Worth Avenue since the '30s. Personally discovered Blass and Trigere to name-drop a few.

Sara Fredericks—Palm Beach
Martha's rival!

WHERE THEY BUY THEIR JEWELS

Tiffany—New York
Where, if you have an extra $7 million, you might be able to talk Harry Platt out of that 128.51-carat diamond.

David Webb—New York
Not as chic as it once was.

Cartier—New York, Hong Kong
They will send you a bag full of gems to leisurely make your selection (if you are a bona fide CC, of course).

Harry Winston—New York
The granddaddy of them all!

Van Cleef & Arpels—Paris, New York, Palm Beach
Winter diamonds from the southern branch are *de rigueur.*

Fred Joaillier—Beverly Hills
All that glitters on glittering Rodeo Drive.

WHERE THEY HAVE THEIR HAIR DONE

Mod's—Paris

Avant garde only. CCs fly in to be crimped, frizzed, and frazzled weekly.

Alexandre—Paris

For the select few (Rothschild, Cabot, d'Uzes, *et al.*). Alex twitters and dawdles for hours it's true, but he still watches over *everyone!*

David Crespin—New York

New "in" place on the East Coast for having the hair carved. The ladies (and a few select men) adore David.

Laurent Gaudfroy— Paris

Ultra-conservative cuts. Most elegant and sophisticated of all!

Kenneth—New York

New York's answer to Alexandre. Patrons of his salon are still the likes of Jackie, C-Z, Ba, Pat, and lots of the other chiclets!

Mr. Lee—San Francisco

Local, but well-known. For the older set only. Lots of reserve!

Nelson Hair Care—San Francisco

Young, sprung crowd. Ricco (the sensation of the West) knows everyone and cuts them dead.

James Reda—New York

For CCs who can't face chauffeurs. James comes to you. Noted for his *personal* touches.

Vidal Sassoon— Chicago, N.Y., L.A., London, etc.

The master only touches his few "favorites," but most CCs have been driven off by too much publicity.

WHERE THEY HAVE THEIR FACES DONE

Arom Runtier—Paris
Most famed dermatologist in the world. Appointments made six months in advance, please!

Harriet Hubbard Ayer—Paris
Royalty only. The *maestro*, Olivier Echaudemaison, has made over Princess Grace, Princess Anne, Princess. . . .

Erno Lazlo Institute for Skin Care—New York
Famous for the "formula for you alone, darling" makeup, Dr. L. personally advises the crème-de-la-crème clientele.

Fabulous Faces—San Francisco
For the chicks of Nob Hill who are too young for Arden.

Charles of the Ritz—Paris
The only branch that the right faces would consider being creamed in.

Elizabeth Arden—N. Y., Paris, Palm Beach, and the rest of the world
An old name but still very much alive with established socialites. The chic one, however, is the Madrid branch. Anthony Clavette, the miracle worker!

WHERE THEY HAVE THEIR FACES LIFTED

Dr. Mar McGregor—San Francisco
For the fabulous "lift-off." President of the American Board of Plastic Surgeons and very much in demand on the West Coast.

Vera Falvy—Institute of Cosmetology, New York
After Converse, it's to Vera. Post-operative care with her strange machines. (She has a real iron to "press out" wrinkles!)

Dr. John Converse—
New York

The master—East Coast
Division.

Dr. Jack Penn—
Brenthurst Clinic,
Johannesburg

The Ivan Pitanguy of
South Africa.

Dr. Ivan Pitanguy—Rio
de Janeiro

Face-lifts, leg-lifts, body-
tucks. The latest craze?
Paring of the bosoms.
Big busts are a no, no
for the topless-
bottomless look.

WHERE THEY FIRM UP

The Spa—Palm Springs

Treatment is fabled.
Eucalyptus steam,
followed by swirling
baths, cold showers, and
massage. Better than a
"youth shot," according
to Walter Annenberg.

Bircher Benner Clinic—
Zurich

Where the rich and
famous eat raw fruit and
vegetables and take *die*
Kur.

Main Chance—Phoenix

Elizabeth Arden's. Filled
with overweight *grande*
dames (Easterners and
Westerners both) from
January to March,
mostly.

Dr. Max Wolf—Miami

Where Palm Beachies go
for the youth shots they
don't need in Palm
Springs!

La Costa—Carlsbad,
California

Attracts the Hollywood
crowd. Dr. Smith sees to
each individual need,
personally.

The Greenhouse of
Neiman-Marcus—
Arlington, Texas

The most expensive at
$1,500 a week (which
includes a visit to the
Dallas Neiman-Marcus
store). Liza (with a "Z")
did her "act" there in
'78.

WHERE THEY FIRM UP *Continued*

Hotel Ixtapan—Mexico

Near Mexico City. The difference here is the local "mud."

Brenner's Park Hotel— Baden Baden

Kingly accommodations, close to the hot springs. A cure-all for whatever happens to all the beautiful people. Granddaddy of all other spas in the world.

La Manga Golf & Health Club—Spain

Newest heady hideout. Saunas, baths, and Iberian massage between flamenco sets.

The Royal Door— Honolulu

In the "Pink Palace" (The Royal Hawaiian) Steve Parker (Shirley MacLaine's "husband") offers "pure, unadulterated luxury."

WHERE THEY BUY THEIR TRINKETS, ANTIQUES, ETC.

Sotheby Parke Bernet— New York, Los Angeles

A $2 million Virginia horse farm, New York penthouses, Knob Hill duplexes, Picassos, Rembrandts, a pair of antique American side chairs ($145,000 for the set)—if you are in the market.

Hotel Drout—Paris

They call it the Parke Bernet of Paris, it seems.

Christies—Vienna, London, New York

The Vienna branch is definitely the "in" place for all Biedemeyer collectors.

YACHTS

Feadship—The Netherlands
The finest crafts in the entire world—up to 110 feet. Priced from $400,000.

DETECTIVE SERVICES

Hal Lipset—San Francisco

The most discreet
private eye in the
U.S.A.—and the one
the right people most
often engage (when
blackmailed!).

MINERAL WATER

Fiuggi—Rome

Best in the world. Non-
gassy but a supreme
digestive, nonetheless.
Imported directly at
$12.50 a liter.

LEGAL SERVICES

F. Lee Bailey—Boston

Until their lawsuit
his references included
the W.R. Hearsts, Jr.

LINENS AND SUCH

Artisanat Libanais—Beirut

Risky, but the best
embroidery anywhere.
Chancy prices, but
"what-the-hell," it's
Beirut.

Pat Crowley—Dublin

The second best
embroidery.

No rundown of such rife, Clout Crowd consumerism can be tallied without a marginal note about "the uptown bag ladies."

When a legend in a lustrous black mink spots a pair of Roger Vivier slippers on the street for only five bucks or an Anne Klein scarf for less, a Cacharel skirt for under fifty, she promptly bags them all (usually in an almost-new Bloomies shopping sack, carried for just such felicitous emergencies).

Shoplifting? Not at all; merely bargain-hunting in New York. And there is nothing even slightly shady about the transaction. Spotting high-fashion merchandise is actually a philanthropic act at most of the charity thrift stores in town, and multiple causes are benefited every time Mrs. Mink goes home with a shot of such wardrobe adrenalin. (It's a secret only her revolving charge account ever knows for sure.)

Husbands (particularly the upper-register caste) are never disabused of the notion that it costs scads and scads of green, darling, just to get the fashion act together! And even if they know it, her friends most certainly will never bring up the fact that the Cacharel she is wearing is remarkably like the one they perused so longingly at the Arthritis Foundation Shop last Tuesday. Only reluctantly allowing it to slip away because it *was* a size 10 and they were not!

Rich women are notorious fashion jades. Rather than be seen wearing the same Dior for another season, they will sell it at a loss or, better still, donate it for an appreciable tax deduction to their favorite charity. Hence the appeal for the myriad band of equally rich but intrepid thrift-shoppers.

And while Salvation Army depots and Goodwill shops proliferate all over Manhattan, there is only one neighborhood where the art of bartering and selling other people's belongings has practically become an art form and that is on *The Gold Coast* (New York's Upper East Side from 59th to 86th Streets).

A bargain-hunting foray of these establishments might conceivably take a canny buyer all day and produce next to nothing, but it is the spirit of adventure that guides a circumspect shopper's course. Starting at The Generosity Thrift on Second Avenue between 69th and 70th Streets, passing through Bargains Unlimited and The Hadassah Shop, and ending at

Salvation Thrift on First Avenue and 91st Street, a dedicated consumer can expect to examine several thousand dollars worth of designer fashions, jewelry, lingerie, and just plain "schmatahs"—some of which just has to be her size!

*   *   *

Since the rich appetite is never curbed by food alone, the "in" restaurants always seem to be those most heavily populated by people who don't give a damn about what they are eating. Besides, "dishing" is a much more vital facet of their social existence.

For most of the rich, however, the dining-out syndrome is validated on two levels. One is being part of the confederacy; if they are seen mixing with their peers in a group situation, it might be inferred that they belong to it (even though they are merely peripheral hangers-on). The other level is a more historical rationale: eating at a chic place is not half so important as being photographed leaving the premises afterward. For posterity's sake, one presumes.

Clout Crowd-watchers should take note of the changing taste in dining habits, however. The "right" people partake of their dinners very late these days: 10:00 to 10:30, while a dozen or so years ago, 8:00 was the absolutely rightest hour to pick up the fork.

A list of some of the chic establishments around the world that remain security blankets for the princely—in any event— follows.

AMERICAN SOLID FOOD

21 Club—New York
Old established CC headquarters.

Edwardian Room, Plaza Hotel—New York
For breakfast only, say the backpackers!

Mike Malkan's Pub— New York
More and more of the "right" people meet here for lunch. Like all those Fords: Henry and Edsel, Charlotte, Cynthia, Anne, and Anne. . . .

AMERICAN SOLID FOOD *Continued*

Lord Gore Club—Vail

Open to members only, but half the world *is* it seems!

P. J. Clarke's—New York

Where Jackie O. eats her burgers, but only after hours. It swings from 2 A.M. on.

The Coach House—New York

Expensive and regional. The old rich like it for "a change," they say.

O'Hara's—Palm Beach

Lobster and la-di-dah!

Sonnesta Hotel—London

Financiers feel at home here.

Bill's—New York

Very drab and very comforting for the old monied who thrive on tradition.

Pepite Marmite—Palm Beach

Dreadful food, tacky decor. But *they* love it just as it is!

FRENCH FOOD

Petite Auberge—Marrakech

Yves St. Laurent and his crowd make it here.

Chez Allard—Paris

Those who know only order the duck with green olives.

La Grenouille—New York

Still the only frog pond for social swimmers!

The Bistro—Los Angeles

The crowd out there calls it "Grenouille West."

Maxims—Paris

The best-peopled parties in the world are given hereabouts.

Grand Vefour—Paris

Still grand, but ugly Americans vie with the waiters for the rudest behavior these days.

Armando's—Acapulco

Meals served 3 hours later than the rest of the world!

Lutece—New York

Sit in the garden *only* at lunch. Eat upstairs *only* after 7.

Vivarois—Paris

Modern and young. Internationally correct.

La Côte Basque—New York

The scene of Truman Capote's new novel—as if you didn't know!

Le Flag—Rio de Janeiro

De rigueur. Once at least!

Laserre—Paris

The rich consider it an obligation, like visiting the Taj Mahal.

La Cirque—New York

Gael Greene was rumored to have had an affair with the chef, Jean Vergnes, and now the rest of New York is having one.

Charley's Saucière—Rome

French food, international faces. Lots of weak chins (which mean royalty!).

ITALIAN FOOD

Orsini's—New York

The lunch bunch time their P.M. departures so *Women's Wear's* photographer will snap them all.

Tratoria Alfredo—New York

Unpretentious. Expensive. The rich have to bring their own wine—and they love it!

La Maschere—Rome

38 different kinds of noodle dishes. Plus 38 millionaires a sitting.

Romeo Salta—New York

It used to be very popular with "them"; now it's reverse chic to appear there without reservations—and insist on a table, anyway.

ITALIAN FOOD *Continued*

San Lorenzo—London
It's the Mayfair set's
Orsini's. Lunch is the
meal they all eat here.

Da Bolognese—Rome
Fettucine, fuss, and lots
of feathers nightly.

*El Toulá—Cortina, D'
Ampezzo*
Après chi-ski.
Wonderful, airy pasta.
But one never eats till
11.

El Toulá—Rome
More candlelight than
Cortina. Sexier crowd,
too.

Ballato's—New York
C-Z said she got there
because of Jackie, who
said Andy Warhol took
her. . . .

*Fattoria—Porto Covo,
Sardinia*
They all fly down for the
fabulous suckling pig.

GRAND INTERNATIONAL CHOW PLACES

Mortimer's—New York
Wall-to-wall face cards
these days. Only name
reservations are
accepted!

Chez Pascal—New York
Very luxe. Overstuffed
with stuffy social types,
but it goes on and on.

*Café Puchine—New
York*
Brand new; owned by
Baroness Pierre de
Neuffville, which carries
built-in clout!

Carol—Cairo
New drop-dead spot.
Jammed with class!

Le Premier—New York
Princess Pahlavi, the
Shah of Iran's twin sister
(and the inevitable
bodyguards), make the
scene here often. Never
alone, however!

Gaddi—Hong Kong
Pink gin and lots of
propriety; the kind of
place elder jet-setters
dote on.

Snaffles—Dublin

Around the corner from
the Shelbourne, well
practically. . . .

La Golue—New York

Very noisy, very natty.
Very in—at the moment.

Burke's—London

Snobby, and the elite
love to eat there.

Melvyn's—Palm Springs

So correct that even
Sinatra eats there.

Nino's—Rio de Janeiro

All the rich *Americanos*
seem to acquire new
escorts here. Feijoada is
spicy, too!

Annabels—London

The last word. Very
upah clahss!

Harry's Bar—Venice

Don't ask for a menu.
The "right" people
don't!

CHINESE

Pearl's—New York

Small and choice. But
Sunday night is the only
night the best people
foregather.

Dragon Verde—Caracas

The best Chinese food in
the whole world, say the
CCs.

GERMAN

Dallmayr's—Munich

Called the Tiffany of the
wurst world. Sells 125
varieties of sausage to
the social set, every hour.

Locke Ober—Boston

Germans come to the
U.S. just to dine here.
Rich Germans, that is!

JAPANESE

Ichiban—Vail

Itsy-bitsy and very ritzy,
too!

Le Spin—Paris

Private club. No
admittance except for
members and guests.
Total *Japonais* experience.

The supplementary news of the rich is that while glamorous restaurants and modish night spots (banished since the early sixties) have returned, touch dancing is still in exile. And the fox trot, waltz, and mambo have gone the way of the African bush safari (delegated to charter-tripping Minnesotans, who bring their battery-charged electric razors and hair dryers with them to the veldt).

The best people now are fleeing the Lester Lanins (polysaturated sounds) and the Peter Duchins (cyclamated syncopation) for disco funk.

And only those places that flash the brightest laser lights and spread the chunkiest glitter on their clientele are considered the in places to be seen these days. Most of these chic-to-chic dancing palazzos are clubs of sorts but hardly of any exclusivity. Disco membership cards (usually running about $150 to $200 per person, per season) carry no prerogatives whatsoever— except a curt recognition by the doorman-bouncer and a slight reduction in the fixed admission charge. Current rates at the hottest disco in New York (Studio 54, unquestionably) range from $6 on weekdays to $7 on weekends. Non-members pay a third more for the same privileges.

A guide to the latest of these late-night culture clinics (both at home and abroad) follows.

WHERE THE RIGHT PEOPLE
SHAKE IT ALL UP

New Jimmy's—Paris

Madame Regine's oldest funk establishment. Still going strong.

Regine's—Paris

The Queen of Disco's latest assault on the Parisian eardrum. '30s decor. Couples only.

King's Club—St. Moritz

Where royalty unwinds after a hard day on the slopes!

Studio 54—New York

The best! Dance floor paved with celebrities nightly. Plus a sprinkling of gays for good measure.

Regine's—New York
A carbon copy of the
Paris number. CCs
abound; next to
impossible for others to
get in!

Jimmyz—Monte Carlo
Regine's gift to Princess
Caroline and the rest of
the young set who were
going bonkers in the
torpid social scene there.

Castel's—Paris
Singles admitted.
Christina O.'s favorite
haunt—before Moscow.

Ice Palace—New York
The latest. Up and
coming.

Maona—Monte Carlo
Regine's also. There was
room for two!

Polaris—Hong Kong
Hottest disco in the
colonies. Full of stir-
fried Americans and
British VIPs.

Infinity—New York
Private. Very. Goes on
long after others shutter.
Clients disco home for
breakfast eventually,
however.

Mark's—London
Annabel's brother, but
the real thing. Disco and
dinner under the same
roof. Elegant and
private.

*Le Bateau—Rio de
Janeiro*
Anything goes.
Especially wild during
Carnivale!

Jackie O's—Rome
"In spot" for people-
watching, but they play
favorites at the door.

Mamounia—Marrakech
Barbara Hutton's only
indulgence.

Twelve West—New York
The crowd is just the
opposite of Studio 54's
here! But "les heteros"
welcome!

*New York, New York—
New York*
For the young CCs.
Stylish; singles!

Chequers—Sydney
Wild and wooly, as the
saying goes. Imported
British rock.

The disco scene might be affecting jet-setters with sacroiliac damage (that might not appear for another decade), says a prominent orthopedic surgeon. But it is evident that they are causing *crise de nerf* for some of their Wall Street clientele that is even more damaging.

Take the case of poor Martin Brummer. President of the Wall Street firm of Packard and Martin, young Mr. Brummer claims that he tried to get into Manhattan's Studio 54 twice during a weekend in February, 1978. On both occasions, though the peripatetic Mr. Brummer showed his membership card, he was denied entry to the club. He finally confronted Studio 54's owner, Steve Rubell, demanding to know what the problem was. Rubell, he says, indicated that he no longer liked the way Brummer looked. With that, Brummer alleges (in a deposition), he was forcibly removed from the premises. Naturally, Brummer has filed suit (for $1 million).

Crosstown at Regine's (one of the disco fraternity), a former member, Tirso Gautreau, also on Wall Street, is suing that club for a like amount. Mr. Gautreau claims that Regine's has been persistently dunning him for a bill dating back to March, 1977, that is not his! Furthermore, he claims that Regine's staff has been bad-mouthing him and blackening his good name all over town!

Saturday Night Fever? It's obviously epidemic.

IX Where They Go!

(Or . . . How to Keep Ahead of the Middle Class)

> Paradise was probably a joy, too,
> until the hoi polloi started to fall in!
>
> Mrs. Cornelius Vanderbilt

Despite a collective reputation for pastel allegiances, "The Rich" hardly enjoy changing their surroundings as often as they seem to be doing nowadays. Barely before a season ends, some new and incomparably chic resort—solely dedicated to the perks of privilege—is heralded as the new "in place" by society's arbiters. And the dowagers and debutantes alike start nervously massing their Vuitton clutches and Gucci totes for instant flight. They abandon their familiar turf, like an army of besieged "Okies," to test the climate of yet another, unpolluted promised land.

The displacement of one firmly established habitat for another, less well tried, has become a way of life for privy capitalists—not out of fickle-heartedness but for what they believe to be the survival of their class structure: *ghetto in excelsior!*

In the past two decades the failure of the jet-set to man the barricades of their pleasure domes (by keeping zoning restrictions high and only selling off parcels of their land to other socially accepted gentry) has resulted in a mass invasion by the middle class, determined to emulate their betters in every dreadful excess. This has culminated in a rash of redoubtably "lost" resorts for the chosen few.

The decline of the Hamptons, Newport, and Palm Beach (rarefied enclaves once but now awash with land developers and proliferating motel managements) has left the old moneyed with a virtually unfillable social void. Even the once impenetrable ranks of The Grand Tour is crammed with economy-class travelers these days—and the old deluxe spas that once catered to only Astors, Morgans, and the like are now booked to capacity by a generation of big spenders whose forebears would not even have considered the possibility of respiration in such rarefied strata. No wonder that the *poor rich* have been forced to become nomads!

150

Just before he gave a final, terrible twist to his 14-carat gold champagne swizzler, Lucius Beebe, last of the elegant livers, was said to have denounced the bottom half of the twentieth century in ringing terms. "A chronological disaster," he averred, gloomily. "A degenerate era not suited to magnificence, elegant amenities, or the spacious way of life I liked to call my own." A gloomy prophet, Mr. Beebe was also, alas, somewhat premature in his deprecation.

In a day when cost accountants are surely inheriting the earth and the law of diminishing returns has made "equality" a dreaded appellation, it is appropriate to announce that a few pockets of taste and refinement still do exist.

As the late Richard Joseph (traveler *extraordinaire* and chronicler of the peripatetic at play) explained to me a while back, "There are certainly some elegant watering holes left in this world; the trouble is they diminish in number just as soon as they are publicized." Curious, but true when one considers how quickly scenery is changed in the upper echelons. Take Acapulco, for instance. Once considered a fabled playground for the "right" people, that posh port of call devalued overnight when an American fashion magazine printed this bit of Acapulciana:

"Rules in this languid lotusland are precise. Meals are three hours later than anywhere else, flesh is for flaunting (bare backs are big this year), and *Formal* on an invitation means the men wear socks." After that appeared, most of the partiers simply abdicated for less promoted parts!

What is most remarkable about all the "new resorts" is their geographic diversity. One hostelry might be smack in the middle of a Mediterranean inlet while another nests under a majestic Alp. But the same names unerringly sign in (again and again) at all the best registers in the world.

Each of these lesser-known resorts zealously guards its guest list to enrich its own cache. No information about habitués' arrivals or departures is ever made available by any of the managements. And an equal air of veiled mystery accompanies all inquiry about future accommodations, rates, or travel arrangements to and from any one of them.

As Joseph described it: "They're like private clubs. No

currency is probably ever passed. Certainly no bills are publicly paid. And the general mien of unabashed opulence is best compared to a stay at the Vatican, where only the Hermes luggage separates the penitent from the dispenser of his absolution!"

What is most surprising to discover about these particular sanctums, however (after a bit of serious snooping), is their prices. Pardoxically, they often charge the "right" people considerably less, for all the indulgent pampering they confer, than some hapless clod staying at the Hilton down the road.

In any event, the 10 ultimate oases of the world (for the moment at least) would appear to be the following establishments:

CALA DI VOLPE: Costa Smeralda, Sardinia, Italy
LAS HADAS: Manzanillo, Mexico
MAUNA KEA BEACH HOTEL: Kamuela, Hawaii
THE TAWARAYA RYOKAN: Kyoto, Japan
DROMOLAND CASTLE: Newmarket, Ireland
HOTEL DU CAP D'ANTIBES: Antibes, France
PETER ISLAND YACHT CLUB: Peter Island,
    B.W.I.
PEPONI HOTEL: Lamu, East Africa
THE PALACE: St. Moritz, Switzerland
HOTEL PUNTA TRAGARA: Capri, Italy

A brief rundown of this covey of resorts follows, with a few of the four-starred visitors to each classic nirvana duly noted:

CALA DI VOLPE (heaven for the Clout Crowd, as Karim Aga Khan obviously conceived it). The true blessing of this *pittoresco paradiso* in Sardinia is its isolation from the rest of the world. Cala di Volpe is still far enough off the beaten track so the moneyed ones have it all to themselves. Price alone (starting at $150 per day) insulates against any packaged tourist invasion. And sheer inaccessibility (private boat or plane are the only means of entry) discourages even the most relentless crush of the *papparazzi* and other celebrity stalkers.

Cala di Volpe is large and low-slung, like an expensive sportscar, and its unpretentious white stone facade barely hints at the degree of "drop-dead" luxury found inside the creamy terraces and arcades. Appurtenances are fabulous, but even they are dwarfed by the absolutely breathtaking vistas—a wraparound landscape that seems to envelop the guest in the majesty of the surrounding mountains and sea.

A dozen years ago, Karim and a few investor pals built a mini-section of the hotel as a quasi-movie setting for private partying. Then the canny Khan persuaded Elizabeth Taylor and Richard Burton to film the movie version of Tennessee Williams's *The Milk Train Doesn't Stop Here Anymore* high above the powdery beaches and aptly named emerald ocean. The movie was prophetically renamed *Boom!,* not for the poor Burtons, who bombed out in it, but for the rest of Sardinia, which flourished as its coast was discovered by resort-hungry CCs.

The "surprise-pink" sand is where the most fabled bodies in the world unbutton their bikinis to skinnydip and perpetuate the tyranny of their tans. Besides Cala di Volpe's private poolside, there are over 80 beaches and cloistered coves splashed along the 35 miles of coastline. And the powers-that-be not only have screened out the local eyesores (poverty pockets and local pimps) but have also dissuaded the local bandits from kidnapping any of the headier clientele.

CCs seen at random include the Aga Khan himself, along with the beauteous Begum Salima, Princess Ira Furstenberg (practically a fixture), Henry Ford, King Constantine of Greece, Count Giovanni Volpi, Jackie Onassis, Diane von Furstenberg, and Lord Snowdon (with various and sundry combinations of players).

LAS HADAS. Braceleting the Bay of Manzanillo on the elbow of Mexico's spectacular west coast and a mere four hours jet throw from Kennedy Airport is this streamlined Baghdad on the Pacific. A gleaming white kingdom perched sky-high atop the Santiago Peninsula where the climate is temperately cool all year round while the water is always warmer than in Acapulco, Las Hadas can be seen shimmering for miles around. And while its ivory towers and galaxy of pavilions and gazebos in the ultimate Mexican/Moorish style has been decried in some quarters as "taco-tacky," make no mistake about the purity of its clients. They are 100 percent *ad valorem* on the hoof!

Rates hover between $50 and $100 a day for the 250 rooms; each suite is a separate aerie with attached garden and mosaic walk. There is a choice of 5 restaurants, 5 nightclubs, an 18-hole golf course, 12 tennis courts, and 3 fresh-water swimming pools, each the size of a blue lagoon. For introverts there are 50 private suites as well (at a slightly higher tariff, of course), each equipped with a secluded swimming pool. The unique thing about this pleasure dome is its whiteness. Everything, literally everything (buildings, walls, furniture, even the snowy beaches below) is virginal and apparently unblemished. Wags say: "It took two billion tons of tin to construct this gold coast and a helluva lot more chutzpah to whitewash it after it was done!" The reference is to the fact that Bolivian mining magnate Don Antenor Patino developed Las Hadas as a pristine meeting place for a few choice friends.

News travels fast in palmy circles, and soon one friend was bringing another along to the exotic playground. At this point, Las Hadas is so solidly booked that no new reservations are accepted for first-time patrons until spring of 1980—or so the scuttlebutt has it along Manzanillo Bay.

Some of the globe's glossiest trotters zoom in and out of Las Hadas from time-to-time (although January and February are definitely considered the optimum months for the bluest skies). The guest list is likely to number these international CCs among the happy throng: Emilio Pucci, Baroness Chantal de Nora, Mary Lasker, Joe and Estee Lauder, Lee Radziwill, Naty Abascol, Betsy Bloomingdale, Mary and Harding Lawrence, and Truman Capote, as well as King Patino and *his* friends!

MAUNA KEA BEACH HOTEL is the very paradigm of Polynesian hideaways, past or present. A hotel of great magnificence, it sets a new standard for the world's best hostelries to be measured against. Here, in unbelievably lavish surroundings (chancily priced from $120 to $325 a day), jaded internationalists can find peace and Zen solitude under the perpetually cloudless skies of Kamuela—or they have the option of golfing the most celebrated and unusual course in the entire world. Constructed at a cost of between $3 and $4 million and covering 230 acres, the fairway follows an ancient effluvial deposit that carved a tract between the blue Pacific on one side and lush jungle gardens, abloom with tropical flowers, on the other.

The hotel itself is a long, horizontal beehive that stretches along the surf. First viewing the place from way out on Kaunoa Bay, the trim cellular structure of the rooms and terraces appears actually to float over the palmed treetops like an enormous hydrofoil. It is estimated that $125,000 was spent decorating each room in the hotel—so CCs have every right to call it their Hawaiian home away from home. Celebrants, who surf, ride, or play tennis (at the 15 grass courts), are such diverse types as John Murchison, Marquessa Villaverde, Doris Duke, Kitty Miller, Frank Sinatra, the Armand Deutches, Barnaby Conrad, and Mrs. Charles Munn.

THE TAWARAYA RYOKAN, Kyoto, unlike sister pleasure palaces is one of the smallest hotels in the world. *Ryokan* actually means "inn" in Japanese, and The Tawaraya is certainly one of the most distinguished (and expensive) imaginable. Over 270 years old and belonging to the same family of gracious entrepreneurs for 11 generations, it is in exactly the same condition (except for obligatory modern conveniences) one might have found it in back in 1707.

Each suite (there are but 19 in all) consists of anteroom, living area, tea ceremony room, private garden and veranda, lavatory, and bath. Guests such as John D. Rockefeller IV and his wife (who spent their honeymoon at The Tawaraya Ryokan) sleep on traditional barley straw pads and *futon* (woven mattresses) taken out of the cupboard at bedtime and arranged on the *tatami*-covered floor.

Other biggies who occupy suites at Tawaraya Ryokan (such as Mrs. Winston Guest, Elliot Richardson and family, Leonard Bernstein, Gloria Vanderbilt Cooper, and Barbara Walters) quickly learn one *never* wears shoes (or even slippers) once they enter their suites. It is considered a lack of grace. Guests also indulge in the national habit of native dress at home. In a *ryokan* one never wears western garments in the privacy of one's home suite, and customary *yukatas* (flowered cotton kimonos) are provided by the management.

All this tradition has a plus side, however. Each suite is blessedly private and has its own assigned housemaid who waits attendance upon her honorable guests with an unbelievable air of servility. The rich and famous definitely like that sort of thing!

The late socialite-journalist Howard Whitman reported: "There is something mysterious about a *ryokan* maid. She darts in and out noiselessly, appearing in her kimono with her tray precisely at the moment when you thirst for green tea; knowing as though by ESP when you open your eyes in the morning; drawing your hot-to-scalding bath exactly when you want it; and appearing at evening to lay out your *futon* with pillow and comforters as though she knew that your eyes were drooping."

The price tag for all this T.L.C. is steep, ranging upward of $150 a day for a suite, which includes private dining and breakfast privileges. And since it takes a computer to calculate the rate of Japan's galloping inflation, rest assured the tariff will be higher tomorrow.

Roosevelts, Biddles, Drexels, Whitneys, Fords, and Mellons are still the starred names on the guest register (week after tranquil week). So, not to worry!

DROMOLAND CASTLE in Ireland is obviously the western counterpart of *ryokan* living. And the baleful news that this former stronghold of the terrible-tempered O'Brien clan was sold to a genial boniface from West Virginia, U.S.A., recently has not diminished its regal patronage one whit. Hardly a day goes by that George and Audrey or Winston and C-Z do not attempt to book a reservation (for next year, of course, when a baronial bedroom-sitting room just possibly might be available).

This castle is a crush scene. And why not? The surrounding countryside is glorious, the service is pre-twentieth-century slavish (read: conditioned to guests' wants), and the food ample, if Irish. No put-down here, but the emphasis is on enormous lobsters and even more gigantic smoked salmons, Kilgarry shrimp by the trencher, and over-cooked beef by the haunch.

156

There are marvelous fresh vegetables all year round, with pots of creamy soups and a parade of buttery pastry nightly that is guaranteed to change a profile in a week. (Your usual castle fare!)

The rich don't come to Dromoland to diet. They do ride a lot, however, and the best horseflesh this side of Deauville is available (at a slight extra tariff) from Burke's stable in Newmarket town—and guides and horses can be delivered practically up to the castle's moat at a moment's notice.

Most of today's Clout Crowd (crammed into city night spots and chic bitsy apartments) long for a touch of green underfoot, and this castle's grounds (some several hundred acres of woodland) provides the right regal ride to convince the jet-setter in the saddle that he is still ruler of the realm, somewhere.

The fee for all this ancestral pomp (and a chance to sleep under authentic family portraits) is hardly staggering. Average modified American Plan stays run between $45 and $85 a day, depending upon the whimsicality of the host and the current cost of peat.

As I have observed, this is an irresistible spot for the clan to forgather, and Dina and Cliff, Tom and Nan, Jean and Amory are all penciled in for spring '79 as of the moment.

HOTEL DU CAP D'ANTIBES is a splendid old bastion of capital in which even newer moneyed types feel remarkably at home. This century-old *splendide* is rumored to have been Fitzgerald's model for the watering place in *Tender Is the Night*, but whether that is so or not hardly matters for this is the kind of withering grandeur that all glittering decadents seem drawn to—like moths to the proverbial flame.

Everything is Grand Prix, Riviera-ravaged; the *boulevardiers* bow and scrape, and the waiters act like musclemen for hire. Even the *demimondaines* speak and sleep in at least five different languages. Eden after the Fall, the beachless "Cap" (as regulars still refer to it) is crammed to its white-stone limits with beautiful bikinied types (of both sexes), who temper their tans at the fabled Eden Rock Pavillion poolside and eat their hearts out as less calorie-conscious diners gorge on the best food to be found at any hotel on the blue coast. Low profile super-rich

(French and Americans, too) feel "the Cap" is a hangout worth anything from $100 to $300 a day for a small suite. Wasn't that Marc Bohan and Phillipe Guibourge? Or Jackie O. and Marissa Berenson, Baron and Baroness Guy de Rothschild, Alexis de Rede, Daniel Wildenstein and Jacqueline de Ribes? The ones in the stringiest bikinis . . . I mean!

PETER ISLAND YACHT CLUB is a very private hide-away that only the rich seem to know about. (Tourists are definitely not welcomed here.)

When Norwegian shipping tycoon Torolf Smedvig first chanced upon a parcel of 540 untrammeled acres in the British Virgin Islands, he declared it a sight for sore eyes. (So like home in Ryfylke Fjord near Stavanger, Norway!) Being essentially a home-lover—and no mean businessman either—he quietly snapped up the island and turned its scrub rock and palmed shores into a posh Scandinavian-style fishing village for play-fishermen only. The Peter Island Yacht Club is his finest hour, an exquisitely appointed 20-room inn plus a mini-marina where other world-weary magnates can tie up their yachts and go native on the most remarkable Nordic cuisine south of Oslo, marvelously appointed service, and the best sun-fishing in the Caribbean. Rockefellers and Rothschilds have been known to cast-off thereabouts. And William Paley, Lady Sarah Roubanis, Lord Orr Ewing, and Geoffrey Knight (developer of the Concorde) are known to drop anchor on occasion.

Prices at the Peter Island Yacht Club are "iffy" (which is a kinder way to phrase the management's reluctance to name a rate), but rumor has it that a small, sunny room can be snagged at about $75 a day. There is a long waiting list for reservations, however, so inflation-watchers take note!

PEPONI HOTEL, just off Kenya's northeast coast, is not nearly as convenient to drop into as a fishing club in the B.W.I., but, on the other hand, a casual remark like, "Have you ever been to Peponi's at Lamu?" dropped squarely between courses at Le Côte Basque one evening soon, could insure you a moment of unstrippable immortality in Clout-Crowd table history.

The few super-intrepid travelers (they usually are well-heeled, too) who have beached down at this coral dot in the Indian Ocean have found the hotel—and the entire island as well—to be, in Yehudi Menuhin's words: "One of the loveliest on earth—a discreet and exquisite paradise!"

Like its biblical reference, the Peponi is terribly pure in its mien. Making no show of being a Hilton outpost, the inn is a low-slung, white porticoed affair, absolutely encircled by lush tropical gardens and a colonnade of coconut palms. There is also a marvelous view of the lapis sea from any given spot on the drinking man's veranda.

The gin is always top grade (Boodles) and the supply of excellent French wines and cognacs a virtual miracle, considering the geography.

Run by an intrepid Danish couple, the Peponi Hotel has a reputation for being something of a *gourmand's* delight— probably due to the mistress of the establishment's formidable skill in the kitchen. A guest book bears this testament from Craig Claiborne, no less: "Let me stay and stay—as cook, bottle-washer, waiter!"

International nabobs, slow to discover this lush idyll, recently have been cutting a tardy swath through the bougainvillea. And such diverse play-folk as Paul Getty, Jr., Gore Vidal, Princess Margaret, Gianni and Marella Agnelli, Mick and Bianca Jagger were recent sign-ins. Prices at the Peponi Hotel vary, depending on the time of year. September to January seem to be the optimum visiting months. Rates begin then at about $55 a day, with meals.

THE PALACE in icy St. Moritz is not where the rich who want the best snow in the world go—for skiing. They choose Utah over Switzerland, hands down. But the Palace Hotel is something else again, a scene that must be made in order to know where one stands in the pecking order of grandees.

Town & Country calls it "the big daddy of winter resorts— oldest, proudest, and most aristocratic." No elite vacation place, winter or summer, tabs loftier names or money. New guests are said to be screened for a year before reservations are confirmed, and the Palace is awash with genteel reminders that the only elegance is the old, established kind, *circa* pre-World War I. There is a Raphael in the Card Room and a staff of over three hundred (better than one servant per guest) to make the gentry truly feel at home. There is even the option (for long-time residents only, I'm afraid) to redecorate one's personal suite from time to time.

As one Regular explained: "It's social suicide to stay anywhere but the Palace. If you do, the right people simply forget that you're alive!!" Living Regulars who pass through the gilded elevator cages include the Shah of Iran and Farah Diba, Henry and Cristina Ford (together once, now separately), Christina Onassis, Prince Charles of Luxembourg, Gunther and Mirja Sachs, Herbert von Karajan, and Rosemary Kanzler.

Prices are unavailable but rumored to be astronomic— beginning at $200 a day, in season.

HOTEL PUNTA TRAGARA is undoubtedly the showoff headquarters of the world. Capri always has been exhibitionist territory. For centuries this tiny, majestic isle has seduced and captured the senses of the rich and mighty. Caesar Augustus surrendered there in the first century B.C. The Emperor Tiberius chose to rule the whole Roman Empire from its cliffs in A.D. 27 and, rumor has it, he threw his abused virgins (of both sexes) into the crystalline waters of the Tyrrhenian Sea on occasion. Today, beautiful bodies bake poolside while visiting barons and film moguls make deals in this elegant pink *palazzo* across the Bay of Naples.

Smaller, more intimate, and more expensive than any other hotel in Italy, the Punta Tragara is also the most romantic. Some of the most celebrated love affairs of our time are said to have been consummated within its discreet confines.

Often referred to as "a view with rooms," this mini-palace has become a life's work project for its owner, suave and dapper Count Manfredi—and there is an air of utter perfection about every physical detail of his establishment. Cornelian door pulls, solid brass hardware agleam in the bath, and the most impeccable service and sensitively prepared food outside of Emilia-Romagna (from which province, it seems, the chief cook and his entire kitchen staff were imported).

Each room of the hotel is actually a suite, and while each has been designed and appointed differently, all have in common majestic stone terraces that overhang the Faraglioni. The Punta Tragara besides having the largest contingent of beautiful paying guests has all of them undressed most of the time. For it is the only hotel on the island with its own natural salt-water pool and interlocking thermal baths and saunas.

Strength-and-health-minded richies swim 200 laps a day and soak up the sun in mixed outdoor solaria afterward. The same pool is used at night for intimate dinner partying—and sometimes moonlight skinnydipping as well.

Everyone who comes to Capri loves to show what he has, as often as possible, it seems. The cast at the Punta Tragara changes with the seasons, but it is often non-stop J. Onassis, Marissa Berenson, Lucia and Helmut Berger, Countess Mona Bismark, Valentino, Graham Greene, Roger Peyrefitte, the Frank Sinatras, and Bob Hornstein.

Prices are chancy; they fluctuate with the lira. Figure on about $175 to $250 a day for suites.

All the rich are so neurotic about being in the right place at exactly the right time that in 1974 *Town & Country* magazine waggishly printed "A People Calendar" as a *Baedecker* of resorts with correct seasonal updates. (It was for those who couldn't bear the thought of being in the right place at the wrong time or in the wrong place at the right time!) Result: 400 canceled subscriptions and a lot of scenery that instantly turned passé! Or so we've been told!

*   *   *

First-class travelers claim that there are at least 15 second-greatest hotels left in the world and, moreover, that it merely will take a return visit by the "right" people to turn them into chic enclaves once again.

To keep the hostelry record straight, we have rated them here (according to our Traveling Correspondent's negative and positive viewpoints) like a *Michelin Guide,* which is to say: mercilessly.

HOSTELRY RATING CHART

No stars = good   1 star = excellent   2 stars = outstanding   3 stars = absolute tops

	Ambience	Prestigious clientele	Food	Guest rooms	Bars	Location
Claridge's, London	**	***	*	**		*
Copacabana, Rio de Janeiro	**	**	*	**	***	**
Fairmont, San Francisco	**	**	**	**	**	**
Gleneagles Hotel, Scotland	***	**	***	**	*	***
Gritti Palace, Venice	***	***	**	***	**	***
Hilton Hotel, Athens	*	**	*	**		
Hotel de Paris, Monte Carlo	**	***	***	**	**	***
Lake Palace, Udaipur, India	**	**	**	**		***
Las Brisas, Acapulco	*	*	*	**	*	*
Little Dix Bay, Virgin Gorda	**	**	*	**	*	**
Mamounia Hotel, Marrakech	*	**	**	**		**
Mandarin, Hong Kong	*	*	**	***	**	***
Marbella Club, Spain	*	***	*	**	**	*
Plaza, New York	***	***	**	***	***	***
Ritz, Paris	***	***	**	**	***	***

X   The Rich Hangups!

(Or . . . What They Do When They Crack Up)

A few years back, a joke circulated about the richest man in the world, who went to visit a psychiatrist for the very first time.

"And what is your problem?" asked the doctor, after the social amenities had been made.

"You tell me."

"I don't understand," replied the medical man, shaking his head.

"Well, it's like this . . . ," said the billionaire. "I have everything a man could wish for in this world. Wonderful children, a faithful wife, good health, too. I have homes in four corners of the globe, and each is staffed with the greatest chef imaginable to prepare my food. I even have a special vineyard that supplies my wine."

"So it's a sexual problem," the doctor coughed discreetly.

"On the contrary. I have this very young girlfriend, you see, who used to be an acrobat. Very young . . . very . . . very. . . . "

"But, my dear man," said the doctor rising, "you should be very happy!"

"Happiness . . . happiness!" groaned the richest man in the world, miserably. "What is happiness? Can it buy *money?*"

It's a gag, of course, but not too far off the mark.

Because the truly wealthy have more of everything than anyone else, it is fair to assume that their pyschological problems are king-sized, too! After a lengthy seminar about money and mental illness, a group of practicing urban psychiatrists in Boston reported that the prevailing neuroses among the rich today are guilt and boredom—with guilt in the foreground of all their ills.

Why do the rich feel guilty?

"Because," as Dr. Howard Shevrin, a University of Michigan psychoanalyst, points out, "their lives have not been sufficiently marked by deprivation. There is a real and nagging doubt about the source of the comforts they enjoy in life that makes them particularly prone to feelings of extreme unworthiness and depression."

The rich kid wonders, why do *I* deserve to have more than others? He feels divorced from the mainstream because his life has not been marked by hardship, so he attempts to break out of his class. To equalize his emotions, he might join the Communist Party or involve himself in the struggle for minority rights, but in all interpersonal relationships he fails. Still inhibited by material possessions, he mistrusts those who are drawn to him. Unable to believe he (and not his money) is the true love object, he usually terminates his relationships and returns to the safe ground of the rich fold (where he can have an expensive nervous breakdown without making waves!).

Psychiatrists claim the young rich constantly test their benefactors' generosity. To determine whether their luxurious appurtenances are genuine expressions of parental affection or mere tokenism, they often indulge in outrageous behavior (such as Patty Hearst's espousal of the S.L.A. philosophy). If the family still accepts them, notoriety and all, perhaps that will convince them they are "truly loved."

But perhaps not. A few well-heeled Weathermen and S.D.S. members, who were disabused of their revolutionary tendencies by short-term therapy, retired from political action entirely as soon as they recognized that their destructive impulses were nothing more than an expression of massive guilt.

In the past, café society was the accepted arena of social rebellion. Playboys and madcap heiresses were cult-figures and exactly what we expected attractive young scions to be. The wacky movies of the 1930s and 1940s established the fun-loving eccentricities of the rich as part of our national heritage.

The recent involvement of the upper classes with radical chic, and their mass conversion to yoga and meditational therapies is less palatable, somehow. EST, TM, transactional analysis, behavior modification, and bio-feedback were all experimented with by guilt-ridden rich dabblers before these commercially viable disciplines filtered down to the middle masses.

Introspection (and the rosy prospect of serenity through deep mysticism) has become such a super-rich preoccupation that many of the wealthiest converts now import personal gurus to assuage their collective karmas. Maharishi Yogi and Swami

Satchidananda (for instance) make a reported 17 to 20 trips a year to the U.S. these days. And they are not the only ashram biggies. Nine years ago, Yogi Bhajan was an anonymous yoga teacher who owned little but a suitcase full of beads. According to *Time* magazine, this "supreme religious and administrative authority of the Sikh religion in the Western Hemisphere" now earns over $100,000 a year in lecture fees and has recently established himself in a well-groomed 40-acre ranch in New Mexico, where his quarters are said to feature a domed bedroom and a sunken bath. That rich zealots are responsible for his rise would appear to be an understatement.

And while the frantic pursuit of Eastern philosophies (Hinduism, Sikhism, Tantrism, Kundalini Yoga, and The Third Spiritual Alphabet) might have peaked in the fever pitch of a few years back, the early seventies will always be remembered, as one wag puts it, "as a time when flush neurotics managed to keep Air India from bankruptcy!"

Though guilt is hardly an exclusive prerogative of the affluent, it appears to surface mainly as a pyschological stumbling block of the *middle-class rich* who inherit most of their resources. The *poor rich* (who are usually *nouveau* in the bargain) are far too preoccupied salting their money away to experience any culpability from the acquisition, and the *really-really rich* are too busy giving great chunks of it away (via foundations and other untaxed beneficences that treble the principal, incidentally) to suffer any guilt pangs at all.

But then the *middle-class rich*, as a group, are the secret inheritors of every major aberrant behavior pattern accruing from *ad valorem*. Dr. Robert Coles, the Harvard psychiatrist, declared that "the common denominator of this group is a sense of 'entitlement,'" which he defines as "a self-judgment about one's position in the world and a self-assurance about the future, at least the social and economic part of the future."

As a privileged child grows up, Dr. Coles says, he becomes increasingly aware that he is "special," that people respect his parents and are sometimes awed by them. Contrary to the myth that the rich are less conscious of money than the poor, Dr. Coles believes that money consciousness is an enormous factor in a rich child's life and that some *(middle-class rich)* children, who hear their parents endlessly complaining about the terrors of taxes, trade unions, and shiftless welfare recipients, grow up fearing for their future.

Some of Dr. Coles's patients (a six-year-old New Orleans girl who was well aware that she would inherit over $500,000 some day and a twelve-year-old boy who lived on an enormous estate north of Boston) worried constantly about living up to their family standards.

"He [father] says that if we don't demand a lot of ourselves, we'll become fat and stupid—and we'll live off our capital and amount to nothing," one child told Dr. Coles. "We will just become *rich* bums, and our children will become *comfortable* bums, and our grandchildren will be *poor* bums of once good families!" With that prospect on their horizon, no wonder the rich crack up with such alarming regularity!

The latest census tabulations indicate that of the 50,000-70,000 suicides that take place yearly in this country, almost 80 percent are committed by persons whose incomes are in the higher brackets. Most definitely suffer from some mild to severe depressive illness that has gone undiagnosed.

The "I-obsessed" super-rich have a harder time finding therapists to unravel their tiny neuroses than you would suspect. For one thing, as a group they share a resistance to transfer their emotions to any member of society (schoolmate, lover, or doctor) less well-born than themselves. And they tend to mistrust all psychiatrists or psychoanalysts unless it can be proven that these doctors are very successful or treat famous patients.

A fairly well-known psychotherapist (who requested anonymity) told of his difficulties treating a very young and beautiful heiress who was so withdrawn she would never remove her sable coat during a therapy session. Though she had been referred by her family doctor (one of the most prestigious G.P.s on Park Avenue), the patient obviously mistrusted him—and would never sit down on his couch until he brought paper towels and covered it for her.

After several months of no progress compounded by long silences and some suspicious appraisals, the patient finally rose one day in the middle of a session and pointed an accusing finger at him.

"I don't really believe that you are Jackie O.'s analyst," she said. When the psychotherapist quickly admitted that he wasn't and questioned where she had heard such gossip, the patient only pulled her sable coat closer around her.

"I know that I am paid up until the end of the month," she said. "But I won't be coming back here any more." Noting his expression of surprise, she paused at the door.

"It's nothing against you. But if I'm going to a shrink, he has to be the best there really is. And I think Jackie O. would have the best!"

Some of the *poor rich* and *middle-class rich* who seek treatment do it because they are bored with their lives or because the notion of therapy has a slightly fashionable cachet to it. (This certainly was truer 10 years ago.) In the main, most rich patients begin therapy after some skirmish with the law or a divorce or because they have done something that their families or friends consider embarrassing or even bizarre. But they are always wary of the parent figure who is trying to communicate with them. Conversely, they seem most secure when the hourly fee they pay is very high!

The steepest hourly rate in New York was set by a fairly young psychoanalyst who deals mainly with rich "problem" children. Oddly enough, when he raised his fee from $100 to $150 a session, his clientele doubled within six months' time.

After some small investigation (totally without the psychiatrists' knowledge or cooperation), we have compiled a small but choice list of the therapists who maintain a heavier workload among the super-rich than most. God help them! The following is a cross-country roster of some of the psychiatrists and agencies that the wealthy seem most likely to unburden themselves to . . . from time-to-time!

WEST

Arnold J. Mandell

Professer at U. of C. (San Diego); co-author of *Brain Chemistry: The Search for Schizococcus.*

George Fuller

Clinical Director of the Bio-Feed-Back Institute of San Francisco.

WEST *Continued*

Daphne E. Bugenthal

Professor at UCLA.

David Shapiro

Lecturer, Dept. of Social
Welfare, UCLA.

Mildred Ash

Author of *Psycho-
analysis and Feminism,*
Berkeley.

Sydney Walker III

Neuropsychiatrist, La
Jolla, California.

Florine Livson

Practices hypno-therapy,
San Francisco.

James Selkin

Director at Denver
General Hospital.

Burton N. Wixen

Author of *Children of
the Rich,* Los Angeles.

MIDWEST

Salvatore Maddie

Professor at U. of
Chicago, specializes in
"existential
psychotherapy."

Charlotte Breytspraak

Well-known New York
analyst, now in
Cincinnati.

Roy Grinker, Jr.

Supervising analyst for
the Chicago Institute of
Psychoanalysis.

Menninger Institute

The most famous mental
health center in the
country, Topeka,
Kansas.

June K. Singer

Specializes in Jungian
psychology, Chicago.

EAST

Vernon Mark

Professor at Harvard,
co-author of *Violence
and the Brain.*

Helen Singer Kaplan

Professor at Cornell and
works with New York
Hospital.

Jay M. Weiss

Does research in psychosomatic medicine at Rockefeller University.

Herbert Spiegel

Invented hypnotic induction profile, NYU, Bellevue.

Marianne Eckardt

Professor at NY Medical College.

Mildred Newman and Bernard Berkowitz

Celebrity analysts. Authors of *How to Be Your Own Best Friend* and *How to Take Charge of Your Life.*

Joan Freyberg

Lecturer at the Post-Graduate Center for Mental Health.

Robert London

Clinical assistant, NYU, Bellevue.

SOUTH

E. Fuller Torrey

Author of *The Mind Game, The Death of Psychiatry,* and *Why Did You Do That?* Washington, D.C.

Edith Weigert

Chairman of the faculty at the Washington School of Psychiatry.

Irving M. Ryckoff

Director of Research and Training, the Washington School of Psychiatry.

John S. Gillis

Professor at Texas Tech University in Lubbock.

Howard Crutcher

Neuropsychiatrist, Dallas.

Lorenzo D' Agostino

Specializes in family counseling, Palm Beach.

Ronald G. Schenberg

Gestalt therapist, Riviera Beach, Florida.

Recent figures on alcoholism indicate that it is the *poor rich* and *middle-class rich* who are most susceptible to problem drinking. In fact, the Senate Alcoholism and Narcotics subcommittee reported (in September, 1976) that the sector of the population where uncontrolled social drinking most often leads to drastic consequences is the leisure class. And, the report continues, families in that stratum of society represent the largest aggregate clutch of alcoholics in America. (Most of whom, more curious still, turn out to be non-career women!)

Ten years ago it was estimated that one out of every six problem drinkers was a woman; now it might be one out of every three. Upper-class matrons are joining Alcoholics Anonymous—in many cases the only source of treatment—at double the rate of the prior decade. And female deaths from alcohol-related diseases among the affluent have risen from 6.3 per 100,000 to almost 8 per 100,000 in the same period.

"Cocktails," as the late Elsa Maxwell is reported once to have said wryly, "are society's only enduring invention!" Stephen Birmingham tells of one lady, decidedly New York Old Guard, who would never even by her worst enemy be termed a drunkard. She liked and was always served a whisky sour by her butler for breakfast. Thus the lady's day began. As it proceeded through the rituals of morning—a glance at the papers, an inspection of the mail—the lady might sip a glass of beer or even a bloody Mary but still feel no pain. At lunchtime, if there were friends or family to table, there most probably would be a pre-luncheon libation—a daiquiri, perhaps, or a white spider (made with vodka and white crème de menthe). With lunch there was always wine, of course, from an anonymous carafe and indubitably a little something after . . . a starboard light, say, which is exactly the same as a white spider but made with *green* mint liqueur. A Scotch or two (though weakened by water) usually carried the lady through the mid-afternoon doldrums until the unrestrained gratification of a properly designated cocktail hour awaited her.

"By drinking light, sweet drinks, sipping them slowly, and spacing them out with certain care," said this observer of the social scene, "this lady, like others of her set, managed never to appear drunk or even visibly tiddly. This helped to convince these people that they were not in the least *addicted* to drink. Yet when, as occasionally happened, they found themselves in a situation where liquor was unavailable, their displeasure became ferocious and their anxiety extreme."

The *middle-class rich,* of course, always have had the option of enjoying their vices in private. Lately, however, it has come to light that a score of posh rehabilitation centers (known as "dry docks" in chic circles) exist to deal with the problems of affluent alcoholics only. Craig House in Beacon, New York, is one of the best known of these private sanitariums, which specialize exclusively in the treatment of wealthy drinkers. Rates start at $1,000 a week.

The Smithers Alcoholism Rehabilitation Unit, a stately Manhattan mansion, once the opulent East-Side home of showman Billy Rose, is reported to have cost $1 million to renovate as a town-house clinic. Its chief benefactor is R. Brinkley Smithers, an enormously wealthy investor who is a recovered alcoholic himself.

The reputation of "Smithers" as a retreat solely for socialites and celebrities who need a discreet city address while drying out was enhanced late in 1977 when Truman Capote showed up drunk for a college lecture in Baltimore and had to be ushered off stage. Reporters covering the event quoted Capote as confessing: "I am a genuine alcoholic," and they mentioned the fact that the wealthy author recently had completed Smithers's 28-day program at $95 a day.

However, according to Dr. LeClair Bissell, director of services (and herself a former alcoholic), Smithers takes poor patients as well.

"As part of our treatment, we want patients to see the spectrum of people [who suffer from this disease], rich and poor, black and white, young and old," she said. "Some people have told us that the experience of being here has altered their lives. One very wealthy man confessed that he had never talked to a black person—as a human being—before! But, for some, the

172

spectrum of different kinds of people has been a problem. We had one rich old lady who didn't want to stay with the others and simply marched out. 'No way,' she said."

One of the lesser-known facts about Smithers is that Joan Kennedy once completed a rehabilitation program there. Mrs. Kennedy is obviously something of an old hand at drying out, but her name is still magic at the admission desk. At least six of the most celebrated alcoholic treatment clinics across the country claim *her* (off the record, of course) as their most distinguished alumna.

Some of the tonier private sanitariums—where Joan Kennedy might have slept—follow.

EAST

Silver Hill

New Canaan, Connecticut. The most prestigious "dry dock" anywhere. Rates from $1,300 a week. But they do accept Blue Cross.

The Palm Beach Institute

Palm Beach, Florida. A cure 'neath the sheltering palms, as the CCs call it. Rates from $575 a week. But the Institute accepts Champus Insurance.

Fair Oaks

Summit, New Jersey. Specializes in corporate alcoholics and top business execs that oversauce. Rates very high, on request only.

South Oaks Hospital

Amityville, L.I., New York. Luxe trade and luxer treatment. Rates $775 for a 5-day detox program. $1,295 a week after, during a rehabilitation regimen of 1 month. Plus $385 for additional testing, not including doctors' fees!

Liveandgrin

Eddington, Pennsylvania. Rich and show-biz-rich hangout. Excellent care. Started by Mercedes McCambridge, ex-Oscar winner and ex-alcoholic, too! Rates from $600 a week.

MIDWEST

Hazelton
Center City, Minnesota.
Reported to have the
best record of permanent
cures. Hazelton is on the
recommended list of the
Menninger Clinic. Rates
not as high as the East
Coast, about $75 to $100
a day. Detox program,
too!

SOUTHWEST

The Meadows
Wickenburg, Arizona
(50 miles northwest of
Phoenix). Where all the
Texas oil biggies go dry.
Rates $90 a day, without
psychiatric or medical
services.

WEST

Las Encinas
Pasadena, California.
Carriage trade only.
Rates higher than Silver
Hill.

Next to guilt, boredom is probably the second most virulent American disease among the very rich.

"Welcome to the banquet of life," the affluent are bidden early on. "But be aware that there is a rigid protocol observed at the feast. *Ennui* sits at the head of the table; *tedium* resides below the salt!"

The ruling class always has put a lot of energy into staving off listlessness. In times past, they invented fetes, hunts, fancy-dress balls, jousts, and even the Crusades to fend off prolonged hours of the "ho-hums."

More recently, to devise newer entertainments, they came up with political intrigues, sex games, gambling, and that most exciting sport of all—war.

As Dr. Estelle Ramey, a professor of physiology and biophysics at the Georgetown School of Medicine declares:

"It takes a lot of ingenuity to stay viable in the face of total leisure. Most of the diversions (that the rich invented for themselves) are now available to large numbers of other Americans, so they don't seem to satisfy any more!"

Rich men go into politics because making money is simply not stimulating enough. Rich women are rushing into industry—taking executive jobs—but then so are not-so-rich women. And the options for singularity fade significantly.

Sufficiency of wherewithal always has been a line of demarcation between the three classes of the rich—and their imitators. But as a resigned acceptance of being "no longer exclusive" becomes a fact of life for most of the moneyed, their diversions have become more heightened emotionally and far, far more profligate financially.

"What separates the men from the boys these days," announced one "with it" socialite recently, "is the denomination of the banknote you snort your cocaine with! Ten- and twenty-dollar bills certainly work, but the really big high is only achieved when you roll up a thousand-dollar bill—or a five-grander—and sniff the stuff through that!"

While most pinstriped Wall Streeters take it from 14-karat gold spoons that double as discreet stickpins, most of the aficionados of "the Cadillac of drugs" inhale it from silver or gold straws from Tiffany: $10 for silver, $50 for gold. But in either case, cocaine (once know as the plaything of jazz musicians and kinky movie stars) is now definitely a habit of the *middle-class rich.*

Among hostesses in the smart sets of Los Angeles and New York (and quite a few in between, as well, according to *Newsweek*), a little "coke," like Dom Perignon and beluga caviar, is now *de rigueur* at Clout Crowd dinners.

"As a matter of fact, the drug is so closely associated with that particular social set," says Dr. Richard Resnick, who is doing research on cocaine under a grant from The National Institute of Drug Abuse, "that CC has become accepted as a term for a heavy user."

"In" party-givers pass it around along with canapés on the cocktail-party circuit; others fill their best Baccarat crystal ashtrays with the stuff—and simply set it on the table, along with the main course. However, lots of hostesses are starting to turn against this practice, according to one jet-setter, "Because they get upset seeing their guests, absolutely stoned, playing games with the beef Wellington and the Scotch salmon!"

Why do the rich take cocaine?

Because it makes them feel so good. The user most often experiences a rush of potency, a surge of confidence and energy that is absent in his preordained dreary social schedule.

"I have such a beautiful feeling when I'm on," says one of the richest and most beautiful women in the *Social Register* when quizzed about her habit. "It's a face-lift for my head!"

Even medical men who have studied the effects of cocaine agree that users generally experience an uplifting sensation that usually is missing in tranquilizers. "It is one of the closest things to a pure feel-good drug," says Dr. Robert Byck of Yale University's School of Medicine, authoritatively.

Luckily, it's still fairly exclusive, too. Though one corporate president at a major broadcasting network had discreet amounts packaged and gift-wrapped for his key employees last Christmas, cocaine is still terribly expensive and illegal, in the bargain.

It also can be lethal if used incautiously. "But so is Arpège if you drink enough of it!" says a *middle-rich* user who defends his habit vociferously.

"Cocaine is *not* a narcotic. It is not addictive, and it causes no withdrawal symptoms whatsoever. It's a helluva lot harder giving up cigarettes, believe me!" says this proponent.

It is definitely harder to buy, yet an estimated 4.8 million Americans (over 30) reportedly tried it last year. And the U.S. Drug Enforcement Administration predicts that the traffic in cocaine undoubtedly will rise (to a $5-billion-a-year business by the end of 1979, is the conservative estimate) if the supply is not checked somehow.

At the moment, the drug sells for between $1,200 and $2,500 an ounce on the street (depending on the degree of adulteration), so it is easily one habit that the rich certainly can retain their snobbish "dibs" on—for the time being.

Less prodigal financially but equally catastrophic emotionally, is another well-to-do crotchet that surfaced under the headline "Bisexual Chic" late in 1974—and seems to be in no danger of obsolescence at the moment. This new social vibration (stemming from endemic boredom, the sociologists report) has made androgyny and the reversal of accepted sexual roles into psychologized chichi.

It probably was inevitable. As "his-or-her" clothes proliferated, hairstyles and role assignments blurred the line between the sexes until they ran together like a Motherwell watercolor. The rich, who have more time for neural disorders, who always are seeking "new and meaningful experiences" to enrich their beige lives, and who are over-democratic in their mass acceptance of all counter-lifestyles (vainly hoping to find some apology for their own), had to make a step in the right direction.

They espoused the trend of sexual overlap in fashion first, didn't they? As late as spring of 1978, Kenzo's *pret-à-porter* fall showing in Paris predicted that by mid-January, 1979, every chic woman in New York would be wearing a tuxedo. "Tucked-front shirt, wing-collar, bow-tie, and enveloping, tapered black pants—a full-fledged trend," announced fashion columnist Ruth Preston. Now, what could be more logical than an out-and-out sex swap itself? If it was certainly gay to be chic, why couldn't it (by some semantic readjustment) be just as chic to be gay? Chicer, in fact!

Whatever Mick Jagger does, the jet-set is sure to follow sooner than later. When faun-like Mick sang love songs to his drummer or dressed in drag for press photographers (as a wartime WAC, of all things), he merely was "pushing the perimeters of sexuality," according to the fashion arbiters. And all the dazzling young men who decorate the poolsides at Las Hadas and Palm Beach pushed in the same direction.

The subculture of feminist groups that brought more and more wealthy women together with their social subordinates for the first time produced not only a rash of upper-class suffragettes for equal rights but a good deal of overt sexual experimentation as well. On Philadelphia's still posh Rittenhouse

Square there is now a feminist club (reportedly in a town house) where women of social standing are able to meet one another without censure or any undue publicity about the nature of their assembly.

In Chicago more than 10,000 wealthy young bisexuals held a congress at The Bistro, a gay discotheque, to raise funds to change the standards of morality in the state of Illinois. And a reported $45,000 was collected in one evening. And though it is not readily admitted (even by the more cognizant townspeople of Tuxedo Park, the richest enclave in Orange County, New York), a Lesbian retreat has been established on one of the oldest and grandest estates in the community. This pleasure dome, ironically enough, was inherited by its present owner, a feminist millionairess, from her paternal grandfather—a militant gentleman who spent most of his life in politics lobbying *against* equal rights for women. And so it goes.

In the liberal atmosphere of money and social position, some of these new bisexuals advocate their lifestyle as the best of all possible worlds. Many social observers, however, see it as another "rich fad," such as polo or collecting movie stars as friends. Only a very small minority, even among the sexually emancipated, seem ready to accept it as wave-of-the-future behavior. Socialite dress designer Diane von Furstenberg, after seven years of marriage, two children, and a revolving door of sexual arrangements, finally left her bisexual husband.

"I couldn't live with it any longer," she explained to her closest friends. "All day long I live the executive life of a man of 45. At night I need at least 5 minutes to be a woman . . . don't you think?"

Amidst the fallout of women's liberation, one begins to hear coming the rumble, the stirring in the bush of other, even more neurotic lifestyles. The bored rich always have had a penchant for mavericks as cult figures they could "groove on," but there never has been such a randy assortment of odd fellows lionized as today. The punk-rock recording stars are edging the pop art boys right off the charts.

There was a time, not too long back, when the most

adventuresome (and certainly the limberest) social climbers claimed that Andy Warhol was the guiding genius and prophet of "our crowd."

"Andy *was* a kind of oracle," Marjorie Reed admitted recently. "But times simply change."

Recalling when Warhol was posed (by Arnold Newman) for a group portrait in *Town & Country* with the New York socialites who were his "very best friends," a sitter recalls the vulpine gathering for posterity:

> When Baby Jane Holzer heard that Marjorie [Reed] was to be in the picture, she refused to pose at all. Marion Javits agreed at first, changed her mind, then finally agreed with strongly expressed misgivings to join the group. A number of Andy's friends refused to be in the same picture with Mrs. [Ethel] Scull. Diana Vreeland, a good friend of Warhol, first said yes, then said no because of the others with whom she would have to share the limelight. Gloria Vanderbilt Cooper refused entirely, saying, "He's been trying for years to do something with me, but there's a necrophiliac quality in his work that goes completely against the grain of everything I do and believe in. I don't want to be associated with him." Others were less punctilious. Sitters included actresses Monique von Vooren and Sylvia Miles; Mrs. Javits; designer Maxime de la Falaise McKendry; Ann Barish, wife of the super-wealthy Miami art collector; Francine Lefrak of the construction company dynasty; and Ethel Scull, Warhol's first patroness, who bought him cheap and sold him high. Incidentally, they don't speak at all these days. So what else is new?

In the actual printed photograph of Andy Warhol (*poor rich*) and the fabled friends who agreed to pose with him, there is a collective look of unrestrained hostility, according to the magazine that published the picture.

"In the middle of it all, ever the observer and relisher . . . recorder of 'people doing insidious, dreadful, horrible things,' sits Andy Warhol, serene, poised, and attentive. He might be the enemy of the people. But in the meantime a great many of those same people are trying—jealously, ferociously, with claw curled and fang bared—to be his friend."

Well, Warhol's out now—and Johnny Rotten and Sid Vicious are in! These newest social replacements are part of a titanic wave of ex-convicts-turned-rock-stars that jet-setters are currently mad about. Rotten and Vicious are part of The Sex Pistols, a British combo ("Jean Genet with electric guitar and reggae bass") that is blessing its way across the upper-crust of everything.

The commonest slogan observed, emblazoned on T-shirts on Palm Beach's Worth Avenue this winter, is "God Save the Sex Pistols!" God save society, too!

Punk-chic is reported to be on the rise among all ages and strata of the rich; crew-cut hair (Marine style) is a must for all the chic ladies in Paris these days. And New York cannot be too far behind them. Dandies in Cardin suits and Meledandri custom-mades wear real (used) razor blades around their throats, according to Eugenia Sheppard, most often strung on chains fashioned of gold safety pins. Safety pins are how one can tell who is punk-chic and who's not! Most of the Paris designer collections (from Kenzo or Laagerfeld) have at least two fashions that are literally held together by safety pins alone. And punk-chic types have taken to sporting them, in their pierced ear lobes and sometimes from the nostril, as well.

The *New York Times* recently announced that there was a new look entitled "nebbish punk" for those who want to look "with it" but are too insecure to give up their Hermes bags. Trinkets included 14-karat gold safety-pin earrings, and pendants that started at $100, were designed by Liz Bader, and sold in Bonwit Teller's jewelry department.

The secret news from Cartier is a reverse chic knock-off of all this punk—a pair of $5,000 paper clips in platinum and emeralds that can be worn practically everywhere.

One cannot catalog punk-chic as a hangup like cocaine or alcohol, quite yet. But give the *rich* time . . . somehow they'll find a way!

XI How They Get Away with Everything

(Or . . . Before You Can Soak the Rich, You Have to Find Them!)

Love is blind. So is the Internal Revenue Service. Happily for rampant capital, the affection of the U.S. government for its richest citizenry always has been respectfully Platonic. And though there have been some lone cries of rape (at The Racquet Club) on occasion, no physical demands are likely to be made this year or in the near future on those 250,000 millionaires who pay little or no income taxes and manage to show up in IRS statistics as low-income individuals because their taxable incomes are so devaluated by expenditure benefits.

To understand this apparent governmental largesse, it is necessary to comprehend, firsthand, the difference between income and wealth—a mind-boggling concept that even the poorest of the *poor rich* rank second to toilet training as instruction for their young.

Most of the blather about who is rich and who is richer (including a healthy portion of this book) focuses on income rather than actual wealth. A man's "wealth" is the value of his individual property and possessions. His "income" is *only* what he earns, *not* what he has, which, if you are following closely, begins to compound the injury!

A rich man's wealth is based not on the funds he keeps in a bank but rather on what he actually owns—the real estate and other cushy objects he has managed to pile up during a lifetime of acquisition: cars, boats, and Lear Jets, for instance. And let us not forget the Picasso in the hall, the Oldenburg on the front lawn, and the assorted Cartier cutlery in the library safe. Oddly enough, most of *that* kind of wealth (showy as it might appear on a list of personal holdings at Sotheby Parke Bernet) is *not* recognized as income at all.

The varied accumulation of "hard-edge" objects does possess a certain value for the owner, however—so don't be too depressed for the Rockefellers. A work of art (or a tract of land, for that matter) still is capable of retaining "unrealized capital gains." But although the piece in question becomes more and more valuable over the years, it can never be taxed until it is sold! That eventuality, however, is highly unlikely because the rich are briefed on inheritance laws and tax write-offs even before they are instructed in the differences between girls and boys.

In a gold-plated nutshell, it is all the untaxable holding they retain that keep the rich richer than the rest of us while maintaining (on the tax rolls) the illusion that they are poorer than many of the so-called middle class.

For example, while the lower third of all families who are bona fide millionaires have 75 percent of the total wealth in the country (according to the 1974 U.S. Census report), they declare only 43 percent of that as taxable income. And while this lower third is ranked as part and parcel of America's ruling class, most of them do not even think of themselves as truly rich. To be frank, they aren't! In a fluctuating economy most of their money is unstable, and only private ownership of wealth makes you solid today. And private ownership (like a private club) is still restricted! Only a tight nucleus of *middle-class rich* and all the *really-really rich* belong. They (virtually untouchable and certainly untaxable) are the string-pullers while the rest of us hustle and jerk to their music.

Most of the big, *untaxed* money in this country is still inherited, passed down from rich father to richer son with nary a jot of dollar depreciation involved in the bequest. One of the principal techniques for bypassing inheritance taxes on huge fortunes is called "Caviar Pie."

"Caviar Pie," according to one of the big tax authorities, entails the split of an enormous family fortune into minute trusts and foundations. Like the toothsome hors d' oeuvre for which it was named, the gross assets of an estate are layered in such a complex manner that the tax people are unable to digest it successfully. And while each trust fund will be taxed (at a rate equal to the size of its provision), the "pie" might be divided to include hundreds of cousins, aunts, and inlaws who share a common interest in the holding as long as it stays intact and under one central director. Small scrapings are made by chary tax men, but the "pie" goes virtually un-nibbled in the final analysis.

Tax reformers in Washington have been lobbying for years for some way to change this unfair transfer of capital—but without much success. One of the suggested schemes is an accession tax. Under such a levy, a wealthy heir would pay the same tax on myriad small inheritances as he now pays on single large windfalls.

Keen weathermen of the proposed alteration in the federal income tax structure take a rather dim view of any major revision in the law, however. How the government chooses by exemption or qualification not to collect taxes is decided, after all, by a committee of elected public officials, who, whether we like to admit it or not, usually are steam-rollered into office with the assistance of the same rich families and mega-corporations they are supposed to be waging war against!

The concensus in higher-echelon tax circles is that apathy keeps the *status* as precisely *quo* as it seems to remain. According to Lester Thurlow, Professor of Economics at M.I.T., most Americans aren't even alerted to the need for a change—no matter how much is written about the inequities of the system.

"Economic debates are merely a subterfuge to stop debate on a realer issue," he points out. "At what point should our society stop its wealth from being concentrated in the hands of a minority? We are quick to pose these questions, particularly for underdeveloped countries, but slow to heed them ourselves!"

And so the rich continue to lead their tax-sheltered lives under the sheltering palms. The number who reap a harvest from expenditure benefits and capital gains is large and growing larger all the time. It is a group consisting of all three classes of the rich, in concert together at last. In this single area there is no discrimination, no class barrier, and no one-upmanship whatsoever. The rich present a totally unified front—motivated to defend (to the last negotiable debenture) all the effective government subsidies they now enjoy.

If you are about to ask when the rich first devised myriad clever ways to avoid paying taxes on their accumulated wealth, forget about it. The moment that opportunistic cavemen held back a little boar's meat after the communal hunt and salted it down for themselves, free enterprise reared its ugly head. The earliest tycoons go back to the Middle Ages when great dukes kept armies of serfs on their land. These tenant farmers tilled the land, provided manpower if the duchy was attacked, and even acted as household staff for the castle, sharing only a bare minimum of the harvest in return for their labors. The serfs also provided the lords with a built-in rationale for not paying a yearly levy to the king.

"Sorry, milord, too many dependents!" is the earliest tax dodge on record.

The concept of a foundation (or a bureaucratic gum-ball machine that, with a little leverage, dispenses favors to the needy artists in the community) had its roots in the Renaissance. Way back then, the Medicis of Florence commissioned a good deal of important art work from Michelangelo and financed the first ballet ever to be performed—to offset some ugly gossip about their political activities (a mass execution of Protestants in the local bailiwick).

The modern funded-foundation (the kind the rich depend upon for economic survival) was created by the U.S. Senate directly before the boom of World War I. The foundation came into existence because journalistic investigations into private monopolies (as well as the exposés of robber barons a decade before) had caused an enormous hue and cry against the concentration of personal power.

The first income tax was set up in 1914—with progressively weighted levies. But before the tax bill could be ratified, the foundation act was hurriedly passed. This provided the rich with a way to funnel their enormous funds (to whom and wherever they chose) without paying burdensome taxes to the government.

In her very funny book about culture barons, Faye Levine points out that when the Foundation Act was first debated in the Senate in 1914, the tone of the debate was often as lofty as the Sermon on the Mount.

Some senators actually considered a proposal that foundation trustees should be approved by a majority vote among the president of the United States, the chief justice, the president *pro tem* of the Senate, the speaker of the House, and the top officers of Harvard, Yale, Columbia, Johns Hopkins, and the University of Chicago! It's amusing to speculate just how long all this highmindedness took to dissipate itself in the rich consciousness since foundations today (64 years later) fund practically anything that seems culturally viable (from early American cookbooks to the preservation of hard-core pornography on film). And don't forget the clutch of once-lived-in rich mansions that the foundation family has opted for museum status!

In 1940 economists identified 13 ranking rich families at the head of over 200 U.S. nonfinancial corporations. These names comprised the fife and drum corps of the *really-really rich* in America: Ford, du Pont, Rockefeller, Mellon, Carnegie, McCormick, Hartford, Harkness, Duke, Pew, Clark, Reynolds, and Kress. By 1978 foundations had increased to 26,000, and the names included such little-wigs as Robert Redford, Racquel Welch, and Jimmy Connors.

A fast look at where the rich cast their bread onto the water might prove enlightening.

Ford: One of the major targets of the Nixon anti-foundation *putsch* of the late nineteen sixties and early seventies (when pressure from the government tried to halt excessive funding of the arts). The Ford Foundation is the largest money-giving machine in the U.S. It's controversial, too! Funding community development projects in New Mexico not long ago, the Ford Foundation was accused by the right-wing press of financing a revolution and by the left of buying off and stifling the radicalism of the leaders. Ford also has been spending about $20 million in nationwide "arts drop." Recipients include the New York City Opera Company, the Joffrey Ballet, the Metropolitan Opera, the New York City Ballet, the American School of Dance, and grants to ballet companies in San Francisco, Salt Lake City, Washington, and Boston. Ford also earmarks funds for Lincoln Center in New York, the Public Theatre Shakespeare Festival, Houston's Alley Theatre, San Francisco's ACT Theatre, and the Art Alliance of Atlanta, Georgia. Besides all that, the foundation is such a heavy supporter of N.E.T. (National Educational Television) that the personnel at Ford Foundation in New York laughingly refer to their employer as the "Ford Foundation Network."

Rockefeller: The foundation of "solid rock," as it is sometimes called by culture vultures, is the second largest benefactor (after Ford) to America's creative industry. The Rockefeller Foundation spread over $70 million to fertilize the arts field during the last 15 years with no hope of a definite harvest. (Music, dance, modern opera, and regional theater are all notoriously slow growers!)

In 1974 the money stopped—or at least it slowed down drastically enough to cause severe anguish for the artistic community and some elation for the drug industry; sales of Valium and Equanil rose sharply during the cutoff. Head arts seeder, Howard Klein, announced the Rockefeller Foundation's decision with much regret! "The culture boom of the sixties is over," he proclaimed, and henceforth the Rockefeller money would be directed only toward substantive projects (such as food, health programs, and the problems of overpopulation in Asia—a far cry from Twyla Tharpe or the Metropolitan Museum of Art).

The Rockefellers, however, always maintained a soft place in their pocketbook for science—so it was not a truly unexpected reversal. Early on, foundation money financed the development of nuclear energy, not to mention the oscilloscope, the electron microscope, and the ultracentrifuge. But while it is often stated that Rockefeller Foundation money saved the lives of countless thousands of German scientists and philosophers during the early days of Hitler's rise, the family has no apparent interest in "saving and preserving" Radio City Music Hall (a Rockefeller Center Corporation enterprise that has been in deficit for a decade) no matter how urgent the cry from militant landmark conservationists and the art deco crowd.

Mellon: The ripest foundation on the vine for art projects at the moment, the Mellon Foundation gave $45 million to various music, ballet, and theater companies in the last decade. But the giving is still on the conservative side; the Old Dominion

Foundation (Paul Mellon's pet preserve) presented over $20 million to his alma mater, Yale; the Andrew W. Mellon Foundation (another family arm) supported the Bronx Zoo, the Metropolitan Opera, and the New York Philharmonic to the tune of $12 million, but *they* are all considered Establishment non-risks, as the saying goes. Two Mellon family members who made chancier investments were Audrey Mellon Currier and her husband, Stephen Currier, who formed the Taconic Foundation in the late 1950s to combat racial injustice. Important contributors to Martin Luther King, Jr., and the civil rights movement in general, the Curriers died in a plane crash in 1967—and Mellon social consciousness seemingly ended with them.

du Pont: Another whiz-bang bestower, some say the du Ponts give away more money yearly than the Rockefellers but prefer not to have their philanthropies bruited about (while the Rockefellers thrive on the glory of giving). Du Ponts control more than thirty banks and operate behind a host of industrial cognomens, from which they divest themselves of a surplus from time to time. So all foundation money funneled through General Motors, Longwood, Nemours, Bredin, Carpenter, Christina, Copeland, Lesesne, Rencourt, Theano, or Andelot can be tabbed quietly as du Pont family enterprises. Most of these foundations support scientific research and areas of medical exploration at the moment (with the bulk of funding channeled into the development of the herbicides they consider vital to the future of the world's food supply. Leading ecologists and environmental groups violently disagree with the experiments, so yet another du Pont family foundation apportions its funds to oceanic investigations by Jacques Cousteau—to offset the negative criticism.

In culture-country the du Ponts are said to have an inordinate concern with self-image and ancestor worship. Many of their art dollars go to the maintenance of a complex "living" museum at Winterthur, not far from the clutch of baronial family chateaux where most of the 1,750 du Pont heirs still make their homes—whenever they are in Wilmington.

Carnegie: "Carnegie" always has been a lovely fiscal-sounding foundation name because it was "firstest with the mostest," as the late Bill Robinson used to say. But after having constructed and funded 2,000 of the most magnificent libraries in the world during the early half of the twentieth century, the philanthropies dwindled. Carnegie Fundation now devotes its funds to individual support of artists and scientists (and zealously guards those recipients against exposure by the press). One well-known foundation concern, of course, is the Carnegie Institute of Technology, which recently aligned itself with Mellon interests to become the Carnegie-Mellon University in Pittsburgh. A long-time supporter of public education, the Carnegie Foundation recently has revived itself to form a commission for public televison.

Pew: Not all foundations are so noble-minded. The Pew family, for instance (affiliated with Sun Oil), is decidedly an anti-art crowd. Instead of cultural events, they opt for hard-line religion. Pew Foundation is a chief supporter of Billy Graham, the Christian Anti-Communist Crusade, and Morality in the Media (a watchdog alert based in evil old New York). Characterized as being "anti-social" and even "Birchite" from time to time, the Pew Foundation has no objection whatever to being known as "an ultra-conservative wing of the Republican right." However, the wing keeps a low profile: no public relations firm and no annual reports!

Eli Lilly Foundation: This foundation (of the monolithic Midwest drug firm) is another donor completely zilched to the cultural scene. More liberal than Pew's crowd, the Lilly Foundation subsidizes Protestant religious hootenannys over here and Radio Free Europe over there! And Matisse is a dirty word never used at a board meeting.

Mott: The Stewart Mott Foundation was formed by an heir to the largest single G. M. stockholder's fortune. It was founded by young Stewart (40) some while back to promulgate his pet interests. Some of these (at random) are universal vasectomy clinics, the Equal Rights Amendment, women's liberation, and Senator Eugene McCarthy's campaign for the presidency (in 1968, 1972, 1976, and presumably in 1980, too!). Mott's foundation, somewhat of a radical stripe, also underwrites the founder's fabled rooftop garden (a working farm atop a New York high-rise), where he is currently raising corn, carrots, and Rhode Island reds.

Hartford: Funded by windfall profits from A & P stores and once exclusively concerned with advanced medical technology, such as laser-beam surgery, the development of pacemakers, and cryogenics (another form of frozen foods, if you come to think of it), the Hartford Foundation certainly has seen better days. Practically bankrupted by the wild speculations of heir Huntington Hartford in show business, publishing, and lately a museum of modern art to challenge the official Museum of Modern Art, the foundation recently announced a hiatus in its public-service activities. Temporarily, one can only hope!

Duke: The Duke Foundation, aside from allocating $6 million to rename Trinity College in Durham, North Carolina, as Duke University, invests about $1.5 million a year in parapsychology and has assembled the largest repository of ESP experiments in the Western World. Doris Duke, on quite a different tack, is assiduously and painstakingly restoring half the city of Newport, Rhode Island, to pre-revolutionary *mint* condition. Which is costing a mint!

Astor: Personally headed by Mrs. Brooke Astor (widow of the founder). The Astor Foundation focuses on ghetto problems and rising juvenile delinquency—in the order of their importance. In existence since the palmy days of New York's real affluence, it helped bail out the city from near bankruptcy some while ago—with no questions asked.

Land: The Land Foundation (Polaroid), one of the newest corporate fists to wear velvet gloves, has given nothing much to the arts, but it recently designated a chunk of building funds to Harvard. Dr. Edwin Land, Polaroid's inventor and president, while not exactly an Old Crimson grad, lives nearby in Cambridge and probably likes the proximity of all that ivy! Recently, the Land Foundation announced itself for clean, safe air—which is probably the least controversial stand a major foundation can assume in a time of crisis.

Other big-gun foundations have a tendency to be iconoclastic, parochial, or even downright quirky about where the money goes. Examples of the free-form foundation start here.

Dr. Coles Trust Fund for Ice Cream for the Pupils of South Plains and Fanwood (New Jersey)

That says it all!

Dorr Foundation

Makes funds available for the painting of white lines along the edges of highways to make driving at night safer.

De Golyer Foundation

Dedicated to the preservation of priceless rare books.

Brown Foundation, Inc., of Houston

Established by Herman and George Brown, wealthy government contractors and friends of LBJ, the foundation supports American Friends of the Middle East (a pro-oil, pro-Arab, anti-Zionist organization) and the Cuban Freedom Committee (an anti-Castro vigilantes group), both backed by the CIA. Other CIA-conduit foundations in oil-lush Texas include: *San Jacinto Foundation; The Marshall Foundation; The Anderson*

Foundation; Hoblitzelle Foundation; Jones-O'Donnell Foundation; and *Hobby Foundation.* All in the name of good works!

Raskob Foundation for Catholic Activities

Raskob, a G. M. executive, was made Private Chamberlain to the Pope in 1928. His money, thereafter, has been funneled into the Catholic Church.

Amon G. Carter Foundation

Founded on American Airlines money, this foundation is dedicated to "experiments in aeronautics" only.

Danforth Foundation

Its assets, composed of Ralston Purina stock, support the financing of college educations for poor boys.

Fleischman Foundation

Like the Land Foundation, it strives for cleaner air, but only in the Lake Tahoe, Nevada, area.

Woodruff Foundation

Its money (from Coca-Cola) fought

desegregation in the South, but it almost "went under" when it funded the posh Atlanta Arts Center, which hardly anyone (black or white) goes to.

Sloan Foundation

While it has financed cancer research and the training of black professionals for years, it recently has diversified into cable television.

Moody Foundation

With the money left it by Willam Moody, Jr., the Galveston insurance and real estate tycoon, this foundation supports only Southwestern concerns (e.g., the Alamo Historical Society).

W. K. Kellogg Foundation

Founded by William Kellogg of the Battle Creek cereal clan, its main objective is aid to graduate students who snap, crackle, or pop!

Sage Foundation

The money of robber baron Russell Sage (thanks to his widow Olivia) supports colleges, hospitals, etc., and publishes a "useful" little booklet—*The Foundation Directory.*

Dorothy Starling Foundation of Cincinnati

Supports the Cincinnati Conservatory of Music.

Kaiser Foundation

Bankrolled with the aluminum fortune, the foundation works with the AFL-CIO in the San Francisco Bay area.

CBS Foundation

Started by William Paley, it concerns itself with young filmmakers who can't get started anywhere else.

H. L. Hunt Foundation

Keeps the late cracker-barrel philosopher's right-wing propaganda campaign going strong.

David & Minnie Berk Foundation

This foundation grants awards for "major achievements in prolonging or improving the quality of human life."

There used to be a popular saying that stated it succinctly: "You can't take it with you!" Well, I would like to amend that aphorism to "you can't if you don't have a good tax lawyer and the right foundation to set up your earthly possessions as a trust after your demise!"

The late Harry F. Guggenheim had a better way. Mr. Guggenheim, an industrialist and philanthropist of sorts, left his entire Long Island estate in Sand's Point as a foundation to exist (exactly as he left it) in perpetuity.

The 26-room Guggenheim mansion, Falaise (a nugget of Long Island's Gatsby era), is maintained as a still-occupied home—that may be inspected by the voyeuristic for $2 a throw. But it may never be peopled by more than eight viewers at any one time!

After checking in at a sentry post just outside the estate, these eight visitors first park their cars; then they are sedately driven the mile to the main house in Mr. Guggenheim's very own limousine (a 1961 Cadillac), which still is driven by Noel Dean, the family chauffeur since 1956.

Along the way, Dean points out the greenhouses, where four gardeners still grow all the plants and flowers that keep the house verdant, and the stables that once housed 25 thoroughbred yearlings. The horses are gone now, but a rustic octagonal aviary remains where pheasants still are bred.

The Guggenheim mansion (designed in the style of a Norman manor house) has all its original furniture and paintings intact—every precious antique still lovingly polished by Ann Dean and Mary Tooker (of the former household staff) daily. In the dining room the table is always set for a formal dinner, and it gleams with silver, crystal, and gold-encrusted china bearing the family crest (a leftover from Mr. Guggenheim's diplomatic days as ambassador to Cuba). All in all, the Guggenheim Foundation is a tribute to what must have been one helluva life.

*   *   *

The money pool is a deep water reservoir. The rich might flounder a bit in its downward current, but they hardly ever lose their footing. *Ad valorem* keeps them afloat—like bars of Ivory soap. Although it must be noted that some capitalists are wanting in the proclaimed "99$^{44}/_{100}$ percent purity." But rich men's crimes are never measured by dollar signs alone. Sociologists regard them as "standard business practices carried one step beyond the farthest reaches of morality." Recently, U.S. Attorney for the Southern District of New York, Robert B. Fiske, Jr., announced that moneyed criminal acts (invariably committed in secret and often the outgrowth of legitimate business) were definitely on the rise. This type of misdemeanor, waggishly referred to as "white-on-white-collar" crime, represents, he claims, more than one hundred times the amount of all money stolen in bank robberies during a year; and that assessment is hardly hyperbole.

"Our economic system is supposedly based on the concept that success results from honest labor," says Fiske. "The notion that rich men who cheat not only get away with their crime but are often rewarded by society weakens the work ethic considerably."

"White-on-white-collar" crime is most often some larcenous act committed by a person of unimpeachable qualifications and high social status in the course of his occupation. The recent brouhaha surrounding the ousting, reinstatement, and eventual voluntary resignation of Columbia Pictures President David Begelman is a prime example of "WOW" crime. Begelman, a $1.3-million-a-year employee who confessed to improprieties involving $80,000 in forged checks drawn on company funds, set off the most widely reported Hollywood scandal in years. But after making restitution (with interest) and enrolling himself in a program of intensive psychotherapy, all charges were dropped— by Columbia Pictures, that is. Superior Court Judge Thomas C. Murphy of California later fined Begelman $5,000 and placed him on three-year probation for having allegedly stolen the money from the movie company. Judge Murphy (who had been beseeched by the Los Angeles County District Attorney's office to sentence the film executive to a three-month prison term as an example to others) refused the request. "I'll not send this man to jail," the Judge declared, "because I don't think such punishment is warranted."

Instead, as part of his punishment, the judge said, Mr. Begelman had agreed to produce a short documentary film on the dangers of PCP, an illicit drug, and show it to high school students and prisoners.

As if to underscore the general acceptance of "crime without punishment" in high places, Columbia Pictures announced that they have signed a new three-year contract with Begelman, hiring him as an independent producer for the studio. His tab, $300,000 per film plus 10 percent of the first $3 million of the gross. On top of that, Begelman (who produced the company's $100 million-plus grosser *Close Encounters of the Third Kind* in 1977) will also receive an undisclosed percentage of the net on all his future projects.

When his canard first came to light and Columbia Pictures blew the whistle on his presidency, the studio stopped paying him his weekly salary and no longer underwrote the rental of his home in Beverly Hills. But all during the period of the fiscal investigation—up to and during his subsequent hearing by Judge Murphy, Begelman retained his original stock options in the company—which at this point are so hefty, it's criminal (if you will forgive the levity)!

John McCandish King, another perpetrator of a biggie "WOW" crime, until recently controlled a fortune estimated at over $480 million. A maxi-tycoon, Mr. King was not only rich but politically prominent, too. A well-known figure at the Nixon White House, he personally acted as the president's representative at the 1970 World's Fair in Tokyo—and was rumored to be a heavy campaign contributor.

King's crime, according to evidence submitted at his trial in 1976, was on an equally lofty plane. He and a business partner, A. Roland Boucher, were found guilty of violating Securities and Exchange Commission laws. It was proved that they defrauded 150,000 shareholders in The Investors Overseas Service Fund of over $126 million by falsely inflating the value of gas and oil resources in the Canadian Arctic.

While Mr. King was sentenced to a year in prison for this escapade, his partner received only seven months. Both men, however, still are apparently free on bail, pending an appeal.

If it is hard to shed a tear for *laissez-faire* oil speculators, cast your eye on another "WOW" crime; this one aimed exclusively at the hapless middle class.

For almost twenty years, raw-boned retirees (and avid late-night TV insomniacs) have been subjected to the blandishments of a better life awaiting them in the sunny Southwest. Lulled to a torpor nightly by "scenes of golden mesas and canyons that sweep the horizon in almost every direction," this mass audience invested (site unseen) a total of $200 million of life savings in parcels of the *Rio Rancho Estates.* The land development, advertised as "a residential community not far from Albuquerque," turned out to be, on closer scrutiny by the Attorney General's office, "semi-arid wasteland."

After years of bilking the public into investing in bogus land schemes, the top officials of Amrep Corporation (purveyors of Rio Rancho and other virtually worthless acreage) were convicted of land fraud in 1977, but no one in governmental circles expects the sentence ever actually to be upheld. And recent American scandals, from Tongsun Park's influence peddling to Lockheed briberies and the unindicted co-conspirators of Watergate, appear to support the notion. A curious gentlemen's agreement between business and government keeps the rate of official corruption and "white-on-white-collar" crime co-equal!

Whitney North Seymour, who was U.S. Attorney for the Southern District earlier, complained vocally that, "The major cause of these rich men's crimes is the attitude of business and professional men. As long as [they] wink at their associates' unethical and illegal practices or, even worse, smile in apparent approval, white-collar crime will be with us!"

Curiously, a campaign launched in California late in 1978 to win freedom for Patty Hearst seems to underscore the U.S. community's apologetic stance in the matter of lofty felons.

Miss Hearst, who is serving a seven-year sentence at the Federal Correctional Institution at Pleasanton, California, and who has about 14 more months to go before she is eligible for parole, is the center of a clemency drive conducted by a group known as The Committee for the Release of Patricia Hearst.

This group, according to the Rev. Edward Dumke, an Episcopalian minister who is its cochairman, has members from all over the state, including Miss Hearst's parents, friends, neighbors, and the four off-duty San Francisco policemen who worked as her bodyguards when she was free on bail.

Curiouser still: Also on the committee is J. O. Tobin, a young man whose father is the President of the Hibernia Bank, an institution Miss Hearst was convicted of robbing at gunpoint in 1976. To forgive is definitely divine in certain circles!

While there have been complaints from the Attorney General's office and from other prosecutors and civil libertarians, it remains a fact that rich offenders are still the only group of convicted felons able to afford the very best legal defense for their actions. And in a survey of "WOW" crimes against comparable acts of larceny, it was determined that rich felons invariably get lighter sentences. Charles J. Hynes, a special state prosecutor in the nursing home scandals that racked New York state a year or so ago, said it most concisely: "Where money is concerned, the punishment does not fit the crime."

A poor little rich caper that barely deserves comparison with white-on-white collar" crime may be worth reexamining here—as a grace note. In 1976, Betty Newling Bloomingdale, wife of the scion of the department store family, was hauled into court for allegedly showing a customs inspector a $500 receipt for a trunkful of designer clothes from Paris.

"You deserve the contempt of society which has served you so well." The judge chided Mrs. Bloomingdale, who having admitted that she cheated "for fun" was truly repentant for concealing the value of her Christian Dior dresses to lower the duty.

Mrs. Bloomingdale's husband, Alfred, a former president of the Diners Club (a company that takes a dim view of any larcenous hanky panky) was at her side for the sentencing.

"$5,000 in fines," announced the Justice soberly, "plus a year's probation for the defendant." And the case was closed.

But the curious thing about this little dido is its inflationary aspect. Each of Mrs. Bloomingdale's frocks cost considerably *more* than $5,000, it was ascertained from the very best source for such tittle-tattle (Dior, itself!). So, the punishment, most definitely *did not fit* that crime—any more than the custom tailoring Begelman received!

*   *   *

If the rich don't get away with everything, they certainly do keep trying. A while back, it was reported in the *New York Post* that while everyone else in the country faces the inevitability of jury duty (along with death and taxes), certain wealthy nabobs never perform this citizenly obligation.

Instead, John and David Rockefeller, along with John Loeb, banker and chairman of Exxon Corporation, Saks Fifth Avenue, and Tiffany's join a host of other fiscal biggies (450 strong and including the presidents of NBC, ABC, Bergdorf Goodman, and Sotheby-Parke-Bernet) to act as members of a very exclusive legal panel: the "Sheriff's Jury."

This conclave, whose membership reads like a veritable *Who's Who* of New York money and whose addresses are Manhattan's Gold Coast real estate (Park and Fifth Avenues, U.N. Plaza, and Sutton Place, with nothing above 86th Street and nothing below 48th) is chosen solely on the basis of fiduciary connoisseurism. Members are (technically) on tap four months of every year, meeting at 4 P.M. Tuesday and Thursday afternoons to determine only matters of financial competency (such as whether or not an elderly millionaire living in an institution is capable of handling his own estate).

Unlike the lower-cholesterol jury system, members of the Sheriff's Jury are not selected at random. Instead, they are nominated for the post (by friends who are already members of the panel) and service is a life term.

A jurist among this cognoscenti has the option of skipping his obligation as a panelist from time-to-time—but he must pay $10 for each day that he misses. There also is an annual dues fee of $370 a year. It costs to be on this jury, you see!

There are compensatory benefits to be reaped nonetheless. For his $370 each juror is treated to an annual get-together in the form of a banquet, held at a prestigious New York hotel. Guests at these gilded affairs are usually judges, politicians, and, more often than not, the Governor—so the money can be considered an investment rather than a levy. There are also very valuable favors for all who attend.

These gifts lately have been assessed as so valuable, in fact (gold watches, Waterford decanters, and Sony Television sets), that there has been talk of scrapping the Sheriff's Jury on the grounds that it is an outmoded aristocratic fraternity rather than a judicial arm. But abolition seems unlikely; too much pleasure and prestige is accrued from the members' associations with one another.

Speaking of the proposed annulment, John Martin, president of Parke-Bernet, pooh-poohed all detractors as merely spiteful or plain jealous. "The Sheriff's Jury," he claimed, "is just another one of the joys of life—that *they* are trying to take away from us!"

*　　*　　*

The rich might get away with a lot in this world, but there is one scam they never seem able to avoid in their plush-lined existences. And that is *le couvert,* or the bread-and-butter charge. As Mimi Sheraton pointed out recently in an article in the *New York Times,* great restaurants (or at least the most expensive ones) recently have begun to add a sur-tax to all the meals they serve—to overcome their rising costs while maintaining the illusion of stable menu prices.

Long a custom in Europe (although abolished by ministerial decree in France in 1967), the cover charge in no way pays for food or replaces a tip for service and definitely cannot be confused with a minimum. Rather, it is a levy for the sole privilege of dining out in glamorous surroundings and one the rich have simply learned to live with.

One interesting facet of this luxurious assessment is where and how it is announced on a menu. The Four Seasons, for example, discreetly lists the charge ($2 for lunch; $2.75 for dinner) at the bottom corner of the bill of fare, but other restaurants display the tariff in more obscure graphic arrangements. At the 21 Club the *couvert* is circuitously tucked between potato choices, and one must truly study the price differential between Candied Sweets Louisiana and *Parisienne persillées* to discover it at all. Le Cirque includes the levy as a "B and B cover . . . 1.00" among the appetizers (directly below Cape Cod oysters 3.75 and slightly to the right of *hors d'oeuvres varie* 4.50). At Restaurant Orsini the information is disclosed in a circumspect italic legend: *"Grissini, white and whole wheat bread and butter seventy-five cents."*

If there are very few complaints at this bit of luxe taxation in the elegant restaurants, it is probably, as Miss Sheraton succinctly states, "because most expense-account customers aren't even aware they are paying the charge and less sophisticated customers who do notice it are too self-conscious to protest."

As I have said, the rich merely accept it as another cross to bear in their already burdened lives. One of those things they just *don't* get away with!

XII   The Eccentric Rich

(Or . . . How They Differ from Thee and Me)

The top honors for being both odd and moneyed comprise a "Hall of Fame" unto itself. Our kooky candidates (past and present) are presented herewith:

Most Penurious

Hetty Green

Wall Street's petty Hetty, *circa* 1900, always wore the same dress (eventually it turned from black to green) and never spent a penny— not even on medical care for her son when he injured his leg (which later had to be amputated). She did, however, leave him $100 million in her will.

Second Most Penurious

Howard Hughes

No question about it!

Most Home-Loving

Alfred Krupp

The great German industrialist so loved the "sound of money being made" that he built his mansion in the middle of his steel works. Fresh linen and clothing had to be purchased once a week as clouds of grit and soot settled over everything.

Most Bone-Picking

John D. Rockefeller

When paying for a chicken dinner with his family, John D. once insisted he was overcharged and called for the plates, meticulously counting each bone, to determine the actual number of chickens they had eaten.

Most Bankable

W. C. Fields

His distrust of bankers led to his depositing sums of money in over 700 banks worldwide. It made him feel safe from "the greed of bankers."

Most Trusting

Honoré de Balzac

The millionaire French author hated the idea of money so much he refused to carry any on his person. (But he had a lot of friends who didn't mind carrying the "filthy lucre" *for* him.)

Most Puzzled

Queen Elizabeth II

She can't carry money either, but then that's just the custom. Instead, she jams her purses with uncompleted crossword puzzles and works on them wherever she goes.

Most Untainted

Henry J. Kaiser

The aluminum king didn't hate money, but he just didn't like to handle "dirty bills." Consequently, his secretary spent a great deal of time running to the bank for freshly printed ones.

Most Florid

Mrs. Alfred Steele

Speaking of dirt. Rich Pepsico board member Mrs. Steele (Joan Crawford to most of us) made it a point upon checking into a hotel to inspect the bathroom floor. If not up to snuff, she would clean it herself!

Most Cutting

Miss Alice Brayton

The late spinster of the Newport clan had such a passion for topiary sculpture that she took great pains (and spent a fortune) to maintain a menagerie of animals: a giraffe, bear, elephant, etc.—all skillfully clipped out of privet in her garden.

Most Pettish

Irénée du Pont

In *his* Cuban garden (before the Castro era) Irénée spent many, many hours teaching the iguanas to come when called. He even taught some to stand at attention!

Most Unfamilial

Sandra and Marian Rockefeller

Sandra, daughter of John D. III, couldn't stand the burden of her family name, so she changed it to Ferry. Marian, daughter of Laurance, makes her own clothes, grows her own food, and lives in a caboose!

Most Capricious

The Warner LeRoys

He (restaurateur) dresses in sequins, and she dresses in $2,000 imitation Elvis suits. *They* spent close to $1 million to make their dining room into a Moroccan "fantasy." After their first party in it, they hated it so, they "threw the whole thing out the next day."

Most Pigheaded

Baby Jane Holzer

When Baby Jane heard that Jamie Wyeth's favorite pig, Den Den, had

204

died, she promptly sent him another, gift-wrapped. The little piggie's name is (what else) Baby Jane.

Most Sybaritic

Bernard Cornfield
48-year-old Bernie, New York mutual funds king, is the swingingest man in Manhattan and Zurich. He "can't seem to get enough of the opposite sex" and parties all night long. He often arrives at work with a young lady on either arm—to party all day long, too. Doesn't seem to care who knows it, either.

Everyone has a quirk or two, but it takes money—lots and lots of money—to allow one's crotchet a full flowering. If the rich seem to thrive on the kinkiness of their personal behavior, perhaps it is because their only true endowment is (as Noel Coward put it) "a talent to amuse."

That the "talent" sometimes is demonstrated by bursts of utter ostentatiousness is a typical preconception we cling to about millionaires, for at the opposite end of the pole, affluent idiosyncracy often takes the form of staggering penury. There is (thank God) no catalog to the endless and whimsical notions that money permits itself . . . but a few more didos speak for themselves.

*   *   *

The late Marjorie Merriweather Post had a rapacious sweet tooth. One of *her* eccentricities was a permanent candy-maker on her household staff (aside from the *sous-chef, saucier,* and pastry cook). At Mar-a-laga, the 115-room cottage she maintained at Palm Beach, Mrs. Post sometimes would hanker after fudge or Turkish delight at 3 A.M.—and a mere tinkle on her house phone always had it forthcoming. Caramels, *penuche,* or bon-bons . . . whatever Mrs. Post craved, it was there! Rumor has it that there were three housemaids (round the clock) paid to be alert whenever the mistress's hot-line rang. Mrs. Post's living expenses once were estimated at about $250,000 a year for her servants alone—and that is obviously what it costs to keep *la vita, dolce.*

* * *

When Mrs. William Woodward, Sr., society's last *grande dame* (hovering around 90, they say), sold her big New York town house and moved into the Waldorf Towers a while back, she reluctantly pensioned off most of her staff. Arthur, her major-domo for 50 years, received a $50,000 trust fund at the parting. Of course her secretary, Miss Bradbury, is still in attendance, and a personal maid of long standing lives in as well, but because of the close quarters at the Waldorf, Mrs. Woodward has to billet another maid at 2 Beekman Place—with a private line for all emergencies.

A special chef at the Towers prepares all of Mrs. Woodward's meals but never her formal parties. Since she still entertains extensively these functions usually are held at favored New York clubs or restaurants. Mrs. Woodward enjoys a degree of personal involvement in all her hospitalities. Some time ago, she gave a dinner party for 80 at El Morocco. The napery and table linens were from her private stock, the flowers chosen from Constance Spry; but the R.S.V.P.s were directed to Elmo's private telephone number. No sweat for Mrs. Woodward!

* * *

Another famous hotel dweller was the aforementioned J. D. MacArthur, often referred to as "America's last extrovert millionaire." The late Mr. MacArthur lived unpretentiously in a rundown resort on Singer Island (about 10 miles north of Palm Beach) that he bought " . . . to beat the servant problem!"

A blunt-speaking man, MacArthur ran his complex business empire (insurance companies, banks, skyscrapers, and conglomerate real estate) from a tiny square table in the noisy coffee shop of the hotel, trading friendly insults with waitresses and whomever else happened by. "I like people," he often averred, "and people seem to like me, too!"

Though MacArthur maintained a hideaway in another part

of his establishment (the Colonnades Beach), it was reported to have been furnished with little more grandeur than most cut-rate motel rooms. Even at his 12,000-acre ranch in central Florida there was no visible sign of luxury. In fact, whenever he elected to stay there overnight, MacArthur usually skipped the main house and camped out in the spare room of his ranch manager's more modest home.

"I used to have a big house in Chicago," he explained, "but whenever I left it—to go on trips—the yardman would let the grass grow and the servants would drink up all my Scotch. I do better living off the cuff!"

* * *

Speaking of self-mades, Claude Canada is one of the country's latest tycoons. Because of the sudden demand for coal occasioned by the energy crisis, Canada netted an incredible $15 million from his strip-mining operations in Kentucky's Pike County (a former moonshiner's haven that has produced more than 40 *middle-class* millionaires since 1974).

Of them all, none is showier and consuming more conspicuously than 57-year-old Canada. Spiffed out in Western-style suits, Lapidus boots, and diamond rings, Canada spends most of his time poring over Rolls Royce catalogs. At the present time, he owns 20 (and is reported to be working his way up to 52, one for each week of the year!).

And though he and Mrs. Canada (lavished in diamonds and furs) eat out often, they never drive. The Canadas cannot abide traffic tie-ups, so they spin off to most places by private helicopter. And although a jet plane is rumored to be on order from Boeing, one can only hope he does not become as incurably addicted to them as he is to "Silver Shadows."

* * *

Mr. and Mrs. Loel Guinness were among the earliest owners of a turbojet. They required such private air transportation because they are far-flung types who pick up and go often—and there is simply no way to travel cross-country on short notice without a private sky-bird at hand. At present, the

Guinnesses have five homes hither and yon, including the Palm Beach house, which is actually a his-and-hers establishment—two full-sized mansions connected by an underground music room.

To get back to the Guinness's turbojet: it is completely decorated with Louis XVI antiques, and Mr. Guinness pilots it on occasion—which sounds like an economy but it's not. The C. A. B. insists that whenever Mr. Guinness flies, a full-time commercially licensed pilot must be aboard the plane—not to mention a maintenance crew of eight as well. But it does *save* time!

*　　*　　*

Joan Payson (who used to own the Mets) not only has a private jet but also a private train and a yacht with a crew of nine, who probably play baseball in their spare time (when the boat is in drydock at her Hobe Sound establishment, come February). But the private-jet set has become so *parvenu* it is hardly worth noting who is flying what these days when so many company presidents (and their families) practically commute in what are laughingly referred to as "corporate" planes. It is also a sign of the times that the Internal Revenue Service (in 1976) allowed the use of yachts and yacht officers as legitimate tax deductions if the crew numbered more than 6 persons. The last newsworthy yacht eccentric, however, was the late Charles Revson, who always maintained 36 crew members aboard the Ultima II, plus 2 physicians and 3 chefs: one French, one Italian, and one Chinese.

*　　*　　*

Though he doesn't fly his own plane or skipper a yacht (as far as we can detect), Malcolm Stephen Forbes might very well be dubbed "the breeziest millionaire of them all." Indubitably no one combines business and pleasure with more panache. In his own words, Forbes spends most of his life "doing whatever there is exciting left to do in this world."

After a lifetime of riding expensive motorcycles and collecting other trifles: Faberge Imperial Easter eggs, presidential autographs, Impressionist paintings, and historic mansions all over the world (the Chateau Balleroy in Normandy, Palais Mendoub in Tangiers, and Battersea House in London, a *pied a terre* on lower Fifth Avenue in New York, a ranch in Colorado, and Zane Grey's fabled fishing camp in Tahiti), Forbes recently discovered hot air.

The 58-year-old owner of the national business magazine that bears his name has become the only capitalist in the Western World to navigate a *balloon* singlehandedly. After several cross-country hops, Forbes attempted the first manned balloon flight across the Atlantic in 1975 and failed—when the premature release of guy lines imperiled the voyage.

"I am not going to try it for a while," the multimillionaire announced after set-backs kept him grounded. "My eldest son, Steve, said, 'If you do it again, Dad, people will consider you a crackpot.'"

In the summer of 1978 when 3 intrepid Americans from the Northwest made the first balloon crossing he had envisioned for himself, Forbes was sanguine. "I'm envious of course, but they got there first," he stated.

Eccentric Mr. Forbes still flies his balloons intracontinentally, however. "I've got five of them. Two in France and three in New Jersey." And he absolutely hopes to try the biggest pond of all (the Pacific) one of these days, "Because I am a doer!" he explained enthusiastically.

*   *   *

Not all millionaires are so flamboyant or high-flying. Douglas Campbell, the early-fortyish founder of D. A. Campbell Company (a large brokerage firm specializing in moving blocks of stock for institutional investors), prefers to marshal his energies for meditation only.

"I am a believer and practitioner of Zen Buddhism," states Campbell, who obviously has nothing against materialism either. In addition to a rambling house in Holmby Hills, California, he maintains a pad at La Costa, another in New York, plus a $50,000 architectural satori in Southampton and a London town house in Mayfair—with a guru in residence.

"My greatest happiness is to share my experiences in

meditation," Campbell says. "Several years ago in India, the High Commissioner of Canada introduced me to his swami—and it changed my life. I invited the holy man with his wife and child to stay with me in London for six months . . . and it really changed my life!" It certainly must have altered Campbell's lifestyle as well. For, from all accounts, they are *still* there!

* * *

Of course, like a lot of less well-heeled folk, some millionaires are happiest in the bosom of their families, living the simple life. Critics of the new rich claim that most of the so-called nouveau-magnates have almost made a fetish of playing down (in reverse-chic terms: homespun exhibitionism!).

H. Ross Perot of the fluctuating Electronic Data Systems dynasty gets his jollies doing light gardening and heading the clean-up squad on the grounds of his modest country establishment outside of Dallas. Frequently he is mistaken for a caretaker by some curious passerby who happens to be a "rich-watcher."

"Say fella, what's a billionaire like to work for?" asked a tourist who collared him putting out some trash recently.

"Well," said Perot, thoughtfully, "not a helluva lot different from you and me."

* * *

Charles Thornton, co-founder and chairman of the conglomerate Litton Industries, is another plain-speaking advocate of the simple, simple life. Mr. Thornton, who drives an eight-year-old car, apologizes that it happens to be a *Lincoln*.

"I used to have an old *Ford* and my wife had the big car, but she decided it was a terrible gas-guzzler, so we switched, 'cause I drive less than she does."

Mr. Thornton and his wife, who live quietly in the Southwest, feel compelled to defend their "conservative" style of life.

"I know there are a lot of people with a heck of a lot less money than we have who live a heck of a lot better . . . but this is what suits us!"

Mr. Thornton's only concession to his phenomenal business success is a small private plane—which he usually pilots himself in the early hours of the morning enjoying the sunrise.

"I can't get anyone respectable to go with me at that hour," he says. "But they're really missing something. When the sun comes up over the desert at dawn . . . Wow! That sight is worth a million dollars!"

*　　*　　*

Octogenarian Henry Crown (the major investor in General Dynamics, Hilton Hotels, and other sundry U.S. hard goods from insurance companies to airlines) despises all overt displays of munificence.

Mr. Crown actively dislikes talking about money, and though his net worth is reputedly about $250 million, he resents being referred to as "a rich man." He buys all of his clothes ready-made (off the rack), owns only one house, and Spartanly divests his life of any excessive pomp or circumstance.

A non-driver for the past 30 years, he does, however, own a Rolls Royce (a present from his wife) that bears a prestigiously low Illinois license plate number: 23. But even the evidence of that over-drive is rarely seen by other motorists. Mr. Crown's automobile only takes to the road at 5:00 A.M. on Sundays. That's when the chauffeur always revs up the car for its weekly 25- to 30-mile exercise run. But Mr. Crown absolutely refuses to be seen in it.

"I'm too embarrassed," he confesses.

*　　*　　*

Dr. Edwin Land, sire of the Polaroid Land camera (a man whom *Fortune* magazine adjudged to be worth between $500 million and $1 billion recently), lives, as we reported earlier, in a most unpretentious, weathered clapboard house in Cambridge, Massachusetts, and to all extents and purposes apes completely the lifestyle of his Harvard-professor neighbors.

"An idiosyncratic fellow," says one close observer of Land's social mien. "The major quirk is his title. You see, he insists on being addressed by *everyone* as Dr."

Although Land has many honorary degrees, he officially never was graduated from any college, and the fact obviously rankles—hence his peculiarity.

Outside of his preoccupation with work, "Dr." Land has few social interests and is reported to be a bit niggardly about spreading his wealth around. On Brattle Street he has the curious reputation for being the only man on the block who refused to contribute to the annual March of Dimes campaign.

* * *

Like Dr. Land, the very richest Americans today often turn out to be little-known tycoons whose business acumen is recognized but whose *persona* has gone virtually unnoticed.

"I have no interest in money at all," says Ray A. Kroc, for instance. Nevertheless, the man who planted the golden arches of McDonald's has managed to pile up more *lettuce* than they shred on "Big Macs" in the 3,795 fast-food locations he guides all around the world.

Most estimates calculate Kroc's wealth at over $600 million, and while he vocally eschews *ad valorem* for *ad valorem*'s sake alone, he is obviously no slouch at enjoying the appurtenances that hamburgers provide (a 210-acre spread in Southern California, a stadium-sized apartment on Chicago's Lake Shore Drive, a 90-foot yacht, 4 helicopters, and a luxurious Florida beach house whose doorbell chimes familiarly, "You deserve a break today" to all callers).

Money-making might not be a prime concern, but his business is the ruling passion of Kroc's life. He is a company man, outside and in, with the gilded gateways he made famous emblazoned on his jeweled cuff links, tie bars, rings, and even on his embroidered, custom-made blazers and boxer shorts.

Kroc does admit to one brand defection however: his favorite food, surprisingly enough, is not the company quarter-pounder. His pet dish, I discovered when I interviewed him a while back, is *osso bucco* (Italian braised veal shanks with saffron rice), which only proves that one man's meat is not always another man's portion!

* * *

The rich, we all know, are often given to bouts of excessive generosity coupled with sieges of co-equal miserliness. The late John Allerton (the Allerton Hotel family), who consistently refused his long-time secretary-companion a raise in pay, (surprisingly) adopted him and left the lucky wage-earner all the Allerton millions and a nice new name to boot!

Nelson Rockefeller is another famous giver and taker. When he and his first wife, Mary Todhunter Clark, divorced a dozen years ago, there was the usual division of properties (in amicable enough accord, it is reported) until it came to the question of custody—not of any children but. of their lavish New York apartment! Mrs. Rockefeller refused to vacate her treasured flat, and the (then) governor declined to relinquish it as well. There were words and revilements, but both ex-partners stood adamant on the issue. Legal adjudication prevailed in the long run, however, and the apartment (a very big one) was split in twain; both former marrieds retained exactly one-half.

The second Mrs. Rockefeller (Happy) was not at all pleased with the division. For one thing, she wanted to be the sole Mrs. Rockefeller in residence at 810 Fifth Avenue. So, to mollify his bride, Nelson Rockefeller did (what we are led to believe all bona fide millionaires do when thwarted) the gallant thing—he bought the building next door. After breaking through the south side of 812 Fifth Avenue, he made a connection with his 50 percent of the original suite, and now everybody lives happily ever after. But it is worth noting, perhaps, that while the Rockefeller servants and the first Mrs. R. still use the old 810 entrance, Happy and Nelson never do. They come and go via 812 *only!*

*   *   *

Just when everyone assumed that zany Texas millionaires were as outdated as roaming longhorns, Stanley (God Bless America) Marsh III came to light. Marsh, barely 40, is in the tradition of early Texas millionaires who first made the state famous. In the old days, there were mavericks such as Jim (Silver Dollar) West, who would order his chauffeur to drive down the main drag of Houston during heavy traffic while he tossed newly minted silver dollars out of the car windows—causing considerable havoc in the streets.

Marsh, who always writes "God Bless America" as part of his name—even on his checks—is best known as the patron saint of "The Great American Dream," which for some lovers of modern art makes a visit to Amarillo imperative—even though the city has never officially recognized the existence of the landmark at its city limits.

"The Great American Dream," designed by a group of revolutionary artists, is a monument of 10 vintage Cadillacs sunk halfway into the Texas soil on Marsh's 10,000-acre ranch; each hood is slanted at the very same angle as one side of the Great Pyramid of Egypt. The monument looks like some twentieth-century Stonehenge, and years from now it might be taken for just that by archaeologists discovering a "new" civilization.

Marsh (who also created a soft pool table on several acres of undulating green grass, complete with huge billiard balls and cue sticks) isn't saying, but you get the idea that he likes the concept of immortality even more than he likes his Texas money!

*　　*　　*

Far from the wooly West, the du Pont family has a tradition with a touch of pop-art as well. Upon turning 17, every male family member is forced to work (at least part time) for his board and room.

This is a long-standing family custom and one that has kept most kinsmen untarnished by "playboyism"; it puts these young inheritors in touch with reality at a more pertinent age than most. Typically, the young du Ponts go into household service. And many a startled Wilmington hostess has hired an extra barman or waiter for a dinner party only to discover that it is a du Pont heir carrying the tray of vodka martinis and the clam dip to the crowd.

To a man, the du Pont boys are uniformly polite at their chores, and though they never wear striped pants or fancy vests at their service, they add a touch of class to a party by greeting guests by their first names. For example, they have been heard to say, "Hello, Uncle Lammot!" or, "So nice to see you again, Aunt Ethel!"

*   *   *

Michael James Brody is at quite the other end of the spectrum of young scions. In 1970, in a spate of grandiose egocentrism, this aspiring 21-year-old rock singer (heir to a healthy real-estate fortune) announced that he was going to dole out all of his personal inheritance of "at least $25 million" to the poor and sick of the world.

Word never quite made it to India, but hundreds of indigent people (taking him at his word) made a pilgrimage to his Scarsdale estate for the beneficence. Thousands more tied up all telephone and telegraph lines to the community for days. Some were merely curious spectators or genuinely intrigued at the idea of a free handout, but a good many more were desperate or maimed people (old and young) who considered charity a true act of welfare in a world of startling non-concern.

But even as young Brody's proposed act of generosity became a matter of public interest and intense media coverage, his patience seemed to wear thin.

"I want everyone out of here, right now!" he shouted at a group of supplicants who queued around his house, "because I'm out of checks now!"

TV cameramen were more demanding than his petitioners. "Here, Michael. Pose with some dollar bills! Throw them now. Right at the people, Mike! No, no, *at* their faces, man! Let's tape it once more!"

As his fame became ingrained in the nightly news programs in every American household, Michael James Brody's goodwill flickered like a worn-out picture tube. He took to sneering at the long lines of people that dogged him.

"I'm sick of hard luck stories," he announced to the waiting press. Emerging from his father's East-Side apartment building in Manhattan one night, he even shouted obscenities at the crowds that braved the cold to wait for him.

"If you don't leave me alone," he screamed, "I'll kill myself—and you'll all die!"

Brody's moment in the public eye was mercifully brief. His wealth, variously estimated at $26 million to perhaps $100 million, was scaled down to something under three—and the family lawyer who handled the estate added that most of it was tied up in trust funds.

Brody did manage to sign a recording contract (with RCA) that was later canceled by mutual agreement. But he still prattled on (quoted mostly in the back pages of tabloids as time went by) about his desire to help the poor people of the world. However, no one took him seriously any more, and he became part and parcel of the lore of rich, flamboyant flimflam men, eventually.

*   *   *

If the rich have maintained an exclusive prerogative on all this eccentricity longer than Karl Marx predicted, rest assured, it was made possible by the tacit approval of two hundred million underclassmen. For in this permissive and unpredictable country of ours, every American maintains that inalienable right to conjecture: "Tomorrow . . . it will be my turn to act crazy!"

If they are right, pity the poor rich!

BIBLIOGRAPHY

Two authors in the bibliography noted below require singling out. They are Ferdinand Lundberg, whose book *The Rich and the Super-Rich* is a bible on the moneyed, and Stephen Birmingham, whose various writings, including *The Right People,* give such enormous insight into the problems that the rich face daily.

Perhaps the biggest *thank you* must go to the New York Public Library—a most incredible institution—just for existing!

Source material was culled from the following publications:

CHAPTER I
New York Times, 229 W. 43rd Street, New York.
New York Post, 210 South Street, New York.
New Yorker, 25 W. 43rd Street, New York.
Time, 1271 Avenue of the Americas, New York.
U. S. News & World Report, 45 Rockefeller Plaza, New York.
Fortune, 1271 Avenue of the Americas, New York.
Esquire Fortnightly, 488 Madison Avenue, New York.
Town & Country, 717 Fifth Avenue, New York.
The Rich and the Super-Rich, Ferdinand Lundberg. New York:
    Lyle Stuart, 1969.

CHAPTER II
Newsweek, 444 Madison Avenue, New York.
Nation's Business, 711 Third Avenue, New York.
*New York Post, New York Times, Time, Fortune, Town &
    Country, The Rich and the Super-Rich.*

CHAPTER III
Los Angeles Times, Times Mirror Square, Los Angeles.
San Francisco Chronicle, 5th and Mission, San Francisco.
Boston Globe, 135 Wm. T. Morrissey Boulevard, Boston.

Philadelphia Inquirer, 400 N. Broad Street, Philadelphia.
Chicago Daily News, 401 N. Wabash, Chicago.
New York Daily News, 220 E. 42nd Street, New York.
Women's Wear Daily, 7 E. 12th Street, New York.
The Right People, Stephen Birmingham. Boston and Toronto: Little, Brown, 1968.
The Very Rich: A History of Wealth, Joseph Thorndike, Jr. New York: American Heritage, 1976.
New York Post, New York Times, Time, Esquire Fortnightly, Town & Country.

CHAPTER IV
1970 U. S. Census of Population, Bureau of the Census. Washington, D. C.: Government Printing Office, 1973.
Oakland Press, 48 W. Huron, Pontiac, Michigan.
Detroit News, 615 Lafayette Boulevard, Detroit.
Kansas City Star, 18th and Grand, Kansas City, Missouri.
The Examiner, 1715 E. 18th, Kansas City, Missouri.
Commentary, 165 E. 56th Street, New York.
Newsday, 1500 Broadway, New York.
New York Magazine, 755 Second Avenue, New York.
New York Times, New York Post, Fortune, Town & Country, The Right People.

CHAPTER V
New York Post, New York Times, Newsweek, Women's Wear Daily, Town & Country.

CHAPTER VI
Harper's Bazaar, 717 Fifth Avenue, New York.
New York Post, New York Times, U. S. News & World Report, Town & Country, The Right People.

CHAPTER VII
Village Voice, 80 University Place, New York.
Psychology Today, 1 Park Avenue, New York.
Children of the Rich, Burton Wixen. New York: Crown, 1973.
The Last Resorts, Cleveland Amory. New York: Harper, 1952.

New York Times, New York Post, Los Angeles Times, U.S. News & World Report, Newsweek, Fortune, Town & Country.

CHAPTER VIII
The Store Cookbook, Bert Greene and Denis Vaughan. Chicago: Regnery, 1974.
New York Post, New York Times, Women's Wear Daily, Los Angeles Times, San Francisco Chronicle, Boston Globe, Time, Newsweek, Town & Country, The Right People.

CHAPTER IX
Travel & Leisure, 1350 Avenue of the Americas, New York.
New York Post, New York Times, Esquire Fortnightly, Newsweek, Town & Country.

CHAPTER X
Harper's, 717 Fifth Avenue, New York.
Good Housekeeping, 959 Eighth Avenue, New York.
New York Times, New York Post, New York Daily News, Esquire Fortnightly, Psychology Today, Time, Newsweek, Harper's Bazaar, Town & Country.

CHAPTER XI
The Culture Barons, Faye Levine. New York: Crowell, 1976.
New York Post, New York Times, The Very Rich: A History of Wealth, The Rich and the Super-Rich.

CHAPTER XII
The Money Motive, Thomas Wiseman. New York: Random House, 1974.
New York Times, New York Post, New York Magazine, Newsweek, Fortune, Town & Country, The Very Rich: A History of Wealth, The Rich and the Super-Rich Right People.

INDEX